D0429768

Assisted Living for the Aged and Frail

Assisted Living for the Aged and Frail

Innovations in Design, Management, and Financing

Victor Regnier, Jennifer Hamilton, and Suzie Yatabe

Columbia University Press
New York

Columbia University Press

New York   Chichester, West Sussex

Library of Congress Cataloging-in-Publication Data

Regnier, Victor, 1947–

    Assisted living for the aged and frail : innovations in design,
management, and financing / Victor, Regnier, Jennifer Hamilton, and
Suzie Yatabe.

      p. cm.

    Includes bibliographical references and index.

    ISBN 0–231–08276–2 (cloth)

    1. Congregate housing—United States. 2. Aged—United States—
Dwellings. 3. Frail elderly—United States—Dwellings. 4. Aged—
Care—United States. 5. Frail elderly—Care—United States.
I. Hamilton, Jennifer. II. Yatabe, Suzie. III. Title.

HD7287.92.U5R44   1994

363.5′946′0973—dc20   93–38639

∞   CIP

Casebound editions of Columbia University Press books
are Smyth-sewn and printed on permanent and durable acid-
free paper.

Printed in the United States of America

c 10 9 8 7 6 5 4 3 2 1

Contents

Foreword

This book is about an emerging type of housing called "assisted living" and the many elements that must be brought together to make it a success. It is about offering choices and personalized care in a manner that enhances the dignity, independence, and freedom of the residents living in these environments.

Assisted living is changing the way long-term care is defined by providing a much needed and desired group housing alternative for frail, older people. In most places where assisted living has been introduced, it has been enthusiastically supported by the community, because it combines housing with personalized assistance, supportive services, and health care.

As a greater number of Americans live longer lives, more of us will focus our attention on how to provide better ways to house and care for our loved ones and for ourselves. Some of us will find assisted living provides a way to make better choices and to maintain greater control of our lives. Others will continue to live at home and may struggle to coordinate a package of services to meet their needs. Still others will be inappropriately or prematurely placed in a nursing home.

Providers of assisted living, policymakers, families, and others involved and interested in this special blend of shelter and personal care recognize it has the potential to benefit many Americans. To make this option a reality throughout our nation we need to encourage quality providers, seek creative financing arrangements, increase public support for low-income residents, and expand public awareness of the resource offered by assisted living facilities. This book addresses all of these topics and other related issues, in a style that is clear and thorough. It provides practical, tested solutions to the challenge of making assisted living work.

ALFAA, the Assisted Living Facilities Association of America, was created in 1990 to promote high-quality assisted living throughout the U.S. ALFAA brings together providers of assisted living, related state associations, those who work with or support assisted living facilities, and other interested groups or individuals including family members and residents. Our principal goal is to enhance the quality of life for those who have chosen or will choose these special environments as their homes.

We commend the authors of this invaluable resource for the important contribution they have made toward helping more frail older people benefit from high-quality assisted living environments. We encourage the readers of this book to heed the lessons that it offers.

> Paul J. Klaassen
> President, Sunrise Retirement Homes & Communities
> Chairman, ALFAA
>
> Carol Fraser Fisk
> Executive Director, ALFAA

Preface

This study started as a descriptive assessment of innovations present in assisted living facilities. During the spring and summer of 1990 we distributed a call for nominations in five categories of innovations. These included; (1) physical and environmental design, (2) finance options, (3) management and operation approaches, (4) services and special program arrangements, and (5) joint ventures between public, private and/or nonprofit sponsors. We obtained lists from organizations involved in the assisted living industry and sent more than 1,700 letters asking facility sponsors, architects, financiers, and management companies to submit materials. We received 130 responses were received with an emphasis in the categories of design, management and financing.

Each entry was read, evaluated, judged, and sorted. Generally speaking, we found it difficult to identify aspects that were truly innovative. In fact, the words *best practice* were substituted in the title of the first report to reflect the feeling that most of the submissions did not describe innovative ideas as much as they described useful ideas appropriate for sponsors to consider.

As we sorted through the submissions, a number of insights about the industry emerged, and we found our descriptive inventory influenced by the types of examples we were analyzing. We were drawn to examples that provided residential-appearing physical environments for the most frail and dependent populations. We searched for R (residential) occupancy buildings in place of the more familiar I (institutional) occupancy buildings, which are more typical of the type used in nursing home settings. We coined the "40/40 rule." This identified settings in which 40 percent of the residents were first- or second-stage dementia victims and 40 percent were experiencing mild to major problems with incontinence.

The principles used to organize the design and management chapters grew out of specific examples we found useful and intriguing. These principles allowed us to group interesting examples around familiar ideas.

In September 1990 I received funding from the Retirement Research Foundation (RRF) to make site visits to twenty projects that were particularly good physical design examples. Many of the photographs are examples of sites that were visited and are used to illustrate ideas identified in the text. We used this opportunity to review the list of self-nominated projects and pursued a second nomination process. During the fall, fifty experts in the area of senior housing were contacted and asked to suggest noteworthy examples of residentially styled facilities that provided in-depth personal-care services to frail older people. One hundred additional project nominations were secured, increasing the total number of projects reviewed to 230.

A Fulbright Western European Regional Research Grant, the Thord-Grey Memorial Award from the American-Scandinavia Foundation, and a grant from the Norway-American Association provided additional funding in the summer of 1991 for the identification and study of 100 innovative European projects in Scandinavia and Holland. This led to another book that compared innovative U.S. and European examples of assisted living (Regnier 1993a).

Since the original publication of this work in 1991, a number of exciting events have affected the future of assisted living. Although the general downturn in the economy has reduced the number of new buildings constructed in 1992 and 1993, there continues to be great interest in the remodeling of existing stock and the development of programs that provide supportive services to independent and congregate housing. Publications by Cohen, Weisman, and Day have made major advances in clarifying issues related to the design of residentially based Alzheimer's facilities. In 1992, the AIA, in conjunction with AAHA, published a design review of forty-three new buildings, seven of which were examples of assisted living. During the summer of 1993 *Progressive Architecture* published a PA PLANS issue on long-term care facilities, which in part demonstrated how far we have come and how much work is yet to be accomplished.

On the policy front, the Center for Vulnerable Populations, under the direction of Robert Mollica, has produced a very useful report examining the experiences of five state governments and reviewing the status of federal programs. The Office of the Assistant Secretary for Planning and Evaluation of HHS commissioned a policy synthesis of assisted living programs and experiences that is in its final draft stage as this publication goes to press (Lewin–ICF 1992). Rosalie Kane and Karen Brown Wilson have completed a study for the American Association of Retired Persons that examines the experiences of the Oregon Medicaid waiver experiment. Finally, in the fall of 1993 the first issue of *Assisted Living Today,* a new quarterly journal dedicated to sharing information between professionals, will be distributed.

It is an exciting time for assisted living. Although there is great enthusiasm for institutional reform, there is equal concern over rushing to define assisted living prototypes too quickly. The most negative consequence of this would be the danger of establishing rigid and narrow regulations that stifle the development and growth of assisted living experiments.

It is our hope that the emphasis on principles and examples in this report will facilitate a better understanding of design, management, and financing, and will further our understanding of this important emerging housing and service type.

Victor Regnier, AIA
Los Angeles,
August 1994

Acknowledgments

This book owes its existence to a number of generous people and organizations who provided their time and the funding for exploring this topic. The major source of funding for the work came from the Administration on Aging (90–AT0386) through the Long-Term Care National Resource Center at UCLA/USC. Later funding came from the AoA-funded National Eldercare Institute on Housing and Supportive Services at USC. Dr. Joyce Berry, commissioner of the Administration on Aging, deserves special thanks for her support of this project and her initiative in encouraging the study of linkages between housing and supportive services. Case study site visits, sponsored by the Retirement Research Foundation, were a later addition to the project. They have added to the book's richness and depth, making many of the concepts more understandable. Brian Hofland of the Foundation saw the benefit of this work and supported its funding. Grants from the Council for International Exchange of Scholars (Fulbright), the American-Scandinavian Foundation, the Norway American Association, the Health Facilities Research Program of the AIA/ACSA Council on Architectural Research, and the Fannie Mae Foundation also supported this work.

We started from a firm foundation based on a careful literature review conducted by Julie Overton, who coauthored a 1989 report that assembled significant past literature in the domains of design, management and financing. Conference presentations at AAHA, CAHA, and ALFAA helped to refine this material by exposing it to broader audiences, who raised interesting and useful questions. However, we owe our greatest debt to the individuals who submitted materials describing 230 projects. They carefully reviewed their work and generously described ideas they believed would benefit others.

The Retirement Research Foundation funding allowed us to pursue a process that involved eliciting the suggestions of fifty senior housing experts. These individuals spent time on the phone suggesting exemplary projects and criteria that we used to define concepts. The site visits clearly involved a major sacrifice of time and effort on the part of a few individuals. The most stimulating was the time spent with Paul Klaassen at Sunrise Retirement Home. Paul cleared his schedule for several days and spent mornings, afternoons, and evenings talking about what he and his spouse, Terry Klaassen, were hoping to achieve in their projects. The enthusiasm and dedication of Carol Fraser Fisk, the executive director of ALFAA, also added to our confidence in the future of this housing type.

Keren Brown Wilson of Rackleff House spent a full day and many hours not only discussing her work but listening and critiquing our thoughts about therapy and design. Subsequently, Keren has been involved in a teleconference, an Eldercare center newsletter article and numerous joint conference presentations. These discussions have helped to further our understanding of how public policy regarding assisted living is developing throughout the United States.

David Hoglund AIA, a principal in the architectural firm of Perkins-Eastman in New York, spent time with us copresenting at meetings and participating in a teleconference. It was through this and subsequent discussions about follow-up projects that many of the ideas first pursued through his work were later examined.

Others who were generous with their time and their thoughts about case studies included Alan Black and Richard Webb of Rosewood Estate, Roseville, Minnesota; Dean Painter of Eaton Terrace II, Denver Colorado; Monte Powell of Daystar, Seattle, Washington; Jan Stenzel and Jerry Taylor of Elder-Homestead, Minnetonka, Minnesota; John Prose and Jakelynn Murphy of Brighton Gardens, Virginia Beach, Virginia; and Stan Hosac of Arizona Senior Homes, Tempe, Arizona.

Case studies involved a number of in-depth interviews. The following people helped us focus on the strategies they had developed to finance projects: Mary Klein and Keren Brown Wilson, from Rackleff House; Dean Painter, from Eaton Terrace II; Bob Benson, of Evergreen Management, and Margaret Michaelis, for the Paddock Kensington; Mary Stevens and Sharon Drier and her staff at the Lincolnia Center; Alan Black, and Deb

Hoglund of Rosewood Estate; Beth Sachs Deely and Charles Pruitt of Woodside Place; and David Peete and Kelly Cook of the Frederick, Sunrise home. Literally hundreds of others have added comments, criticisms, insights, suggestions, and ideas through informal discussions and telephone conversations.

A special thanks to the architects that helped us with case study drawings. These include for *Rackleff House:* Chilless Nielson of Portland, OR; *Eaton Terrace II:* Oz Architecture, Boulder, CO; *Paddock Kensington:* Galpin, Claccio and Associates, Ltd., Minneapolis, MN; *Lincolnia:* Herbert Cohen and Associates Chartered, Washington DC; *Rosewood Estates:* Arvid Elness Architects Inc., Minneapolis, MN; *Woodside Place:* Perkins Eastman and Partners, New York City; and *Sunrise of Frederick:* Beery, Rio and Associates, Annandale, VA.

We are indebted to the people who have helped us and hope that this book will benefit them and others who will find information here that will help make a difference in the lives of older people residing in assisted-living environments.

Assisted Living for the Aged and Frail

1. Defining Assisted Living

The term *assisted living* has entered the lexicon of housing developers, non-profit sponsors, and policymakers as a description of both a housing type and care philosophy for older, frail people. Assisted living has been used to differentiate this housing type from conventional board-and-care and personal-care housing. Personal-care housing has been highly influenced by medical models of nursing care, whereas board-and-care homes are small-scale, family-style arrangements that often operate without professional management assistance.

Assisted living housing represents a model of *residential* long-term care. It is a housing alternative based on the concept of outfitting a residential environment with professionally delivered personal-care services in a way that avoids institutionalization and keeps older frail individuals independent for as long as possible. Care can consist of supervision with minor medical problems, assistance with bladder or bowel control, and/or management of behavioral problems resulting from early stages of dementia. In an assisted living environment all these problems are managed within a residential context. This type of housing fits between congregate housing and skilled nursing care.

Nine Definitional Qualities

A shared definition of *assisted living* has yet to materialize. In fact, a recent policy study initiated by the Office of the Assistant Secretary for Planning

FIGURE 1.1. *Assisted living residents are between 82 and 87 years of age and need help to maintain independence:* Some have ambulatory difficulties, while others are beginning to experience some mental confusion.

and Evaluation of the Department of Health and Human Services (Lewin-ICF 1992) cites seven different definitions that vary widely in their specificity. The following definition used by the Assisted Living Facilities Association of America (ALFAA) captures many salient dimensions: "A special combination of housing and personalized health care designed to respond to the individual needs of those who need help with activities of daily living. Care is provided in a way that promotes maximum independence and dignity for each resident and involves the resident's family, neighbors and friends."

For this publication we have chosen to specify qualities that suggest a loose normative interpretation of what assisted living promises to be. Although few facilities of this type meet all these criteria, they provide appropriate targets sponsors can aim toward as they conceptualize highly supportive, humane residential housing for the mentally and physically frail. Assisted living facilities should:

1. *Appear residential in character*—the form and character of assisted living should be derived from the house and not the hospital.

2. *Be perceived as small in scale and size*—the setting should be as small as it can be without sacrificing monthly cost stability and the capability of providing twenty-four-hour assistance.

3. *Provide residential privacy and completeness*—the housing unit should be complete, with a full bathroom and kitchenette.

4. *Recognize the uniqueness of each resident*—the contribution and needs of each resident should be expressed through a program of activity and a plan for services that treats each person as a unique individual.

5. *Foster independence, interdependence, and individuality*—the focus of care should be on self-maintenance with assistance. Residents should help themselves and one another.

6. *Focus on health maintenance, physical movement, and mental stimulation*—the setting and its programs should stabilize decline, improve competency, and build reserve capacity.

7. *Support family involvement*—a care-giving partnership should be forged that shares responsibility for resident well-being with family members rather than vesting the facility with total responsibility.

8. *Maintain connections with the surrounding community*—the setting should integrate rather than isolate residents from community resources and contacts.

9. *Serve the frail*—residents should be older people in danger of institutionalization, with basic personal-care needs for assistance.

Two Typical Resident Profiles

The typical resident of an assisted living environment is often a frail female in her mid-eighties. Typically, she is in danger of institutionalization because of a decline in competency and an inability to organize the necessary network of services to live independently. There are two typical profiles.

The first is the older cognitively alert, physically frail individual. She often suffers from a debilitating disease like arthritis, hypertension, or diabetes and has problems carrying out the activities of daily living (ADLs). She may require assistance in bathing, toileting, grooming, ambulation, medication supervision, and/or eating, but her need for service stops short of twenty-four-hour nursing care.

The second profile is the physically able but mentally frail individual experiencing the first stages of dementia. She often has difficulty comprehending the environment and may be easily confused, or lost even in familiar surroundings. As the disease advances, restlessness, irritability, and behavioral problems can develop.

Assisted living settings generally serve both of these types of individuals, although in many facilities individuals with dementia are clustered in one area, so that problems caused by wandering can be controlled without placing the resident in jeopardy or disturbing others. There has also been strong interest in the development of residential settings that serve only early to moderately impaired dementia residents. In a recent book Cohen and Day (1991) review case studies of several facilities of this sort. Although they are based on a residential model, many of these dementia facilities have generally not been labeled as assisted living, even though they attract the same type of mentally frail individual as facilities that mix both the mentally and physically frail.

Neither of the profiled resident types belongs in a nursing home. Disorientation and restlessness, like incontinence, are not good enough reasons for institutionalization. However, American social and health policies have generally abandoned individuals with these problems, assuming that nursing home placement was the only alternative. In other cultures the desire to keep individuals independent and out of nursing homes for as long as possible forms the cornerstone of a comprehensive long-term care program. In the United States these individuals must either enter a nursing home or fend for themselves in the community.

Assisted Living Concepts

The nursing home is conceived physically and operationally around a model for providing care that has its precedent in the hospital building type. Nursing home staff members are trained in conformance with a medical model of care. Building codes used to construct these settings are based on institutional occupancies. The configuration, exiting/egress requirements, and general safety considerations of nursing homes are derived from codes that traditionally have been used to build hospitals. In essence, the nursing home is a transformation of the hospital environment. Assisted living, on the other hand, has its typological roots in residential housing and can be interpreted as a transformation of the mansion house, country villa, or bed-and-breakfast hotel.

Understanding the differences between assisted living, personal care, board and care, and skilled nursing is one of the best ways to imagine what assisted living has to offer as an alternative to current arrangements. Keren Brown Wilson, who has been instrumental in developing several assisted living facilities in Oregon, has articulated four concepts that underlie the philosophy of assisted living (1990).

1. Create a Place of One's Own

This concept assumes each resident has a single occupied housing unit with a private bathroom and kitchen. As simple and straightforward as this concept may seem, personal-care settings are often designed like skilled nursing arrangements. Many do not have lockable doors, and often are double occupied.

2. Serve the Unique Individual

The needs of physically competent but mentally frail residents differ from those of individuals with severe chronic arthritis who have difficulty dressing. A range of resident competencies requires a service response that is flexible and individualized. Basic services include meals, housekeeping, laundry, and assistance with activities of daily living. A monthly resident assessment should monitor, update, and adjust the level of service provided by the facility, factoring in the contributions made by the resident's family and friends. The ability to custom-fit service levels to the specific requirements of an individual resident is an important aspect of a flexible assisted living model.

3. Share Responsibility Among Caretaker, Family Members, and Resident

Shared responsibility in decision making allows residents and their families to participate in goal setting and to negotiate an appropriate care plan. This approach contrasts with the typical "one-size-fits-all" model of service provision, where every resident receives the same set of services regardless of competency or the level of family assistance provided. The direct participation of family members in assisted living is viewed as an important emotional and instrumental aspect of providing care.

State regulations can complicate the involvement of family members because the formal care provider has a legal responsibility of meeting state-mandated standards of care. Facilities, understandably, are reluctant to share responsibility with family members when the institution can be held legally liable for the care and monitoring of residents. Such regulations, although well intended, can erode the relationship between resident and fami-

FIGURE 1.2. *A lock on the door symbolizes privacy, independence, and autonomy:* A simple feature like this can represent the philosophical difference between skilled nursing and assisted living.

ly members. Involving the family in helping activities is also an effective strategy for establishing increased personal communication.

4. Allow Residents Choice and Control

Older residents should be able to exercise a full range of choices and should control their destiny within a supervised, service-intensive, assisted living housing arrangement. Unfortunately, allowing residents to decide simple matters such as when they would like to take a bath or which entree they would like for dinner is often impossible in nursing homes. In fact, some administrators consider choice a luxury that is impossible to achieve with frail individuals of diminished competency.

Responding creatively to the issue of choice and control reinforces one's sense of self-esteem, self-reliance, and self-respect. One factor limiting this concept is the approach used to offer choice. For example, allowing a resident to choose between two dinner entrees by placing them in front of her is relatively easy compared to reading a menu and making a more abstract decision. Strategies for providing choice should consider a resident's capacity for abstract decision making.

Regulatory Barriers to Assisted Living

Three primary regulatory impediments constrain the options and possibilities associated with assisted living: state regulations, building code restrictions, and zoning and land use restrictions.

State Regulations

State regulations affect the manner in which care is provided. These typically limit the participation of family members in negotiated care arrangements and often establish institutional requirements that reduce the autonomy and independent decision-making capability of the older person. Nursing home regulations are often mandated, rather than being based on performance standards. This makes it difficult to respond creatively and comprehensively to care-giving needs.

Assisted living becomes controversial when it challenges the state-mandated indicators of competency used to clarify who belongs in skilled nursing facilities. When Oregon's assisted living regulations were introduced, the idea that incontinent residents with behavioral problems could be better supported within a residential environment was greeted with skepticism. Subsequent experience with the program has been eye opening (Kane and Wilson 1993). States that have drawn a line between the social and health care models of care provision are discovering how fuzzy that line can be.

Regulations Define the Care Philosophy

Human service professionals concerned about the effects of regulation on care provision have joined policymakers aware of rising long-term care costs and families who feel alienated by an outdated system that discourages their participation. These groups now question the appropriateness of conservative "tip-over" regulations establishing an early point at which the older frail can no longer be cared for in a residential facility and therefore must be moved to a nursing home. Providing proof of the arbitrary nature of these regulations is the range of home health services currently being provided to older persons in their homes.

Added to this are the experiences of other countries, such as Denmark and Sweden, that have placed moratoriums on the development of nursing homes and are actively advocating the delivery of health services to older people in residential environments. Nursing homes in these Scandinavian countries are viewed as subacute hospitals, where only the most severely impaired belong.

Redefining the appropriateness of institutional environments for mentally and physically frail older residents can be compared to the revolutionary changes hospitals have experienced in the last five years. During this time, medical technology, cost-conscious regulations, and new outpatient treatments have totally redefined the idea of the "required hospital stay" for a range of procedures. The same radical change could be experienced in nursing homes if regulations were updated and funding was provided for assisted living as an alternative to the nursing home.

Building Code Restrictions

The second set of regulatory constraints comes from building codes modeled after hospital building and safety requirements. These affect a range of decisions, from the finishes allowed on corridor walls to the size and configuration of a resident's room or its distance from a centralized nurses' station. In general, building codes for these occupancies facilitate staff movement and efficiency and give little consideration to the needs of the older person.

Despite the interest of consumers in the development of humane, supportive, homelike environments, code restrictions that ensure safety often encourage the institutional layout and appearance of these environments. Building codes and overly cautious attitudes regarding infectious disease control favor the specification of commercial low-maintenance materials, whereas changes in technology and updated fire-fighting techniques are often not reflected in revisions to outdated code requirements.

In Europe the majority of housing is sponsored by public and nonprofit entities. This increases public trust, making it easier to implement more experimental arrangements. In the United States, public concern about nursing home abuse has encouraged more stringent code interpretations. Although these codes may result in safer facilities, they do so at the cost of creating dehumanized environments.

Zoning and Land Use Regulations

The third major regulatory constraint involves land use and zoning codes that hamper the integration of housing for the frail with surrounding neighborhood land uses. Zoning codes for nursing homes fall within institutional zoning categories. These are not considered compatible with commercial or residential land uses. Furthermore, mixed-use statutes are rarely encouraged. More often than not, housing for the frail stands alone in the community, isolated from other people and places in the surrounding neighborhood.

European approaches are quite different and often involve combining

FIGURE 1.3. *A window between the kitchen and a protected light filled atrium encourages social contact:* This feature also allows light to enter dwelling units of the Captain Eldridge House in Hyannis, MA from two sides.

land uses, such as a senior center, housing for the frail, a home health agency, an outpatient medical clinic, a restaurant, and a physical therapy rehabilitation center. Mixing uses opens the setting to a broad range of users and connects it to the community, giving it relevance to a number of constituents (Regnier 1993). In European housing, home-care services are often coordinated out of service houses, which provide housing to the frail as well as services to help older people stay in their own homes. For a more detailed description of this European building type and how it compares with U.S. facilities refer to the book *Assisted Living Housing for the Elderly: Design Innovations from the United States and Europe* (Regnier 1994).

Sorting out the necessary from the discretionary code requirements is complicated. Recently, the Retirement Research Foundation funded a clearinghouse demonstration project to examine overlapping codes and advocate for standards that are user centered and less institutional. The project, sponsored by the American Association of Homes for the Aged, is called the National Registry and Clearinghouse on Aging and Environmental Design Codes. Affectionately known as the "code busters," project members have been busy centralizing information on federal and state design standards.

How and Why Assisted Living Has Evolved

A number of personal, institutional, societal, and financial factors have caused a rethinking of how to provide care to older frail persons. The following nine factors have been instrumental in stimulating the development of assisted living as a housing and health care alternative.

1. Increasing Numbers of Older Frail

Demographic growth caused by increases in cohort size and longevity have swelled the ranks of those over age eighty-five. Middle-series projections by the U.S. Bureau of the Census anticipate a doubling of the over-eighty-five population in the twenty years between 1990 and 2010, followed by another doubling in the next thirty years (2010–2040) (U.S. Senate Special Committee on Aging 1991). This 300 percent predicted increase in fifty years is considerable but may greatly underestimate the potential increase. Guralnik, Yanagishita, and Schneider (1988) argue that pending biomedical breakthroughs and advances in disease prevention and therapy could continue the 2 percent decline in mortality experienced by the United States in the last twenty years. Using this assumption, their forecast shows the over-eighty-five population spiraling from 3.3 million in 1990 to 23.5 million in

2040. This represents an over 600 percent increase in the size of this vulnerable age group.

Medical advances, hip replacements, and new physical therapy regimens are allowing the old to live longer, but more of this oldest-old-age group cannot live independently without personal assistance. Increased demand for quality long-term care services has been the result. Also, outspoken demands of a more affluent oldest-old-age group have forced sponsors to upgrade services and environments to compete for attention.

2. Availability of Community-Based Long-Term Care

New communication technologies and the proliferation of "portable" nursing services delivered to individuals in their own residential environments have brought into question the need to institutionalize individuals for economy of scale and safety. If a service network can be established through a consortium of efforts provided by adult day-care settings, home-delivered services, family members, friends, and paid support personnel, why is it necessary to institutionalize the older person? Some board-and-care providers are using home health agencies to serve the medical care needs of residents, thereby supporting this trend.

3. Increasing Costs of Nursing Home Care

An overdependence on nursing home beds resulted from federal and state government subsidy polices that ignored assisted living as an alternative. Now skilled nursing costs are rising along with the general costs of medical care. There continues to be a growing gap between what Medicare/Medicaid pays and the real costs associated with providing quality skilled nursing care. Increasing costs have also caused many older people to forestall admission to a nursing home or to pursue alternative arrangements. A recent *Wall Street Journal* article (McCarthy 1992) described a creative approach taken by one older incontinent woman who, through the purchase of a $429 monthly bus pass, had lived on a Greyhound bus for four years in an attempt to avoid placement in a nursing home.

4. Questioning of the Inevitability of Institutionalization

Efforts to deinstitutionalize mentally impaired individuals in the early 1970s introduced the concept of community-based services. This reform called into question the need for costly and dehumanized institutional arrangements for the mentally ill. The role of skilled nursing facilities in the system of long-term care services has also been questioned by a number of socially progressive European countries. These cultures question the assumption that institutionalization is an inevitable outcome of growing old and becoming frail.

5. Evolution of New Alternatives Between Congregate Housing and Skilled Nursing

Assisted living has evolved out of the need to develop a supportive housing alternative between congregate care and skilled nursing care. As a result, creative alternatives between the housing and health care models of service provision have proliferated. Assisted living arrangements within continuing-care retirement communities (CCRCs) in the United States were first developed to save facilities the added cost of institutional care for frail residents who did not require skilled nursing. CCRC providers recognized how inadequate congregate housing and skilled nursing models were in dealing with the range of resident competencies that exist between these two environments.

The creation of adult day care, the expansion of home health services, and the development of special residential facilities for Alzheimer's victims characterize physical and programmatic responses to the interest consumers and care providers have in "partitioning" this gap. These new housing and service responses take into account the overall strengths of the frail older person and prescribe a service plan and environment that maximizes independence. In previous years nursing home placement might have been the only option available.

The recognition that a number of creative alternatives can be employed to fill the gap between congregate housing and skilled nursing care has created options and choices unavailable five years ago.

6. Phasing Out of Intermediate Care

The increasing average age and frailty level of individuals admitted to nursing homes have contributed to the shift away from intermediate nursing care. Because they often do not require skilled nursing services, many residents receiving intermediate care can be better served in the community. Moreover, the reimbursement rate for intermediate care is far less than that needed to cover costs in labor-intensive institutional environments.

7. Relaxation of State Regulations

Regulations at the state level have been moving in the direction of vesting greater responsibility and authority in the community health care providers who work with older people. Consultants and health care specialists from the community often treat both acute and chronic health care conditions within an assisted living environment.

Public housing providers have also found it necessary to deliver support-ive services for older people who have aged while living in independent housing built in the late 1960s and early 1970s. In the past these housing providers have handled resident needs for a higher level of care on an iso-lated basis, by moving such residents to board-and-care or skilled nursing arrangements. However, as the public housing stock has aged, the overall frailty level of the residents has increased. Today many government assisted housing projects accommodate very old frail populations who have aged in place (Struyk et al. 1989). Many providers are therefore searching for ways in which they can offer personal care services. Some have established "ser-vice overlays" that deliver a range of services to residents living in their own units. However, some providers have opposed this move, considering it in opposition to their mission statement.

In some states home-delivered services coordinated by an external agent such as a home health agency have been used to circumvent official policies that limit the housing authorities' role. In these settings health care services are provided by a home health agency and social and supportive needs are met through the housing lease.

New interpretations of state regulations have allowed these alternatives to develop and have given assisted living facilities the freedom to coordinate more intensive health-related services.

8. Greater Consumer Demand for Alternatives to Institutionalization

Providing older people and their families with a dignified residential alter-native to institutionalization is perhaps the most powerful reason for the popularity of assisted living. Whereas older people generally fear nursing homes, their families view nursing home placement with guilt and disdain. A move to a skilled nursing facility is considered a last step to be made only after an older family member has experienced an accident or all alternative service provision efforts have failed. Many consider the nursing home a pre-lude to increased dysfunction and death.

The scandals that have affected the nursing home industry and the low level of financial remuneration provided to sponsors give cause to fear the worst. Many of the current cohort of older frail persons have placed their own parents in nursing homes. They are therefore frequently aware of the problems that characterize these arrangements; some have vowed to avoid their own institutionalization at any cost.

Because older consumers are increasingly aware of the choices available and the problems associated with traditional skilled nursing care, the search for alternatives has increased. Children are happy when they can locate an alternative to skilled care and thereby avoid the humiliating and dehumanizing experience of institutionalization for their parent(s).

The same consumer and policy pressures that have led to the emergence of assisted living as a long-term care alternative have also provided impetus for the reform of nursing home design (Hiatt 1991). However, the rigid regulations and narrow interpretations of appropriate therapies and environments to be used in this building type in the United States have stopped the application of many creative ideas. Without radical rethinking and bold new initiatives efforts to reform the nursing home are destined to be only band-aid solutions to a much more serious problem.

9. Increased corporate interest in creative housing alternatives for older frail people

Major hospitality providers, such as the Marriott Corporation, have combined their experience in hospitality environments with a new interest in the provision of health and social services. Many of these new corporate models (the Brighton Gardens Marriott prototype, for example) include some nursing beds that complement a larger collection of catered living and personal-care residential units. Although corporations view skilled nursing care as foreign to their corporate culture and past experience, they see assisted living as similar to other high-service hospitality arrangements with which they are more familiar. Because of this, assisted living is considered a logical model for innovation and investment. Corporate providers have targeted their efforts toward designing care environments that resemble residential homelike settings and yet are professionally managed.

The preceding factors are among a host of other considerations that have led to the development of assisted living arrangements. Clearly, the demographic imperative; consumers' interest in finding an institutional alternative; the desire from a public policy perspective to reduce the costs of long-term care; and the need to develop housing that embraces the family and

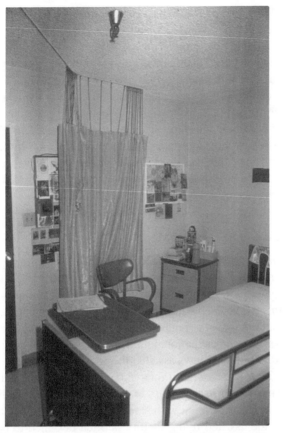

FIGURE 1.4. *The nursing home is based on a health care not a housing model:* Double rooms with hospital beds and privacy curtains define this lifestyle.

provides opportunities for risk management, case coordination, and shared responsibility will continue to encourage the refinement of assisted living models.

Precedents from Continuing-care Retirement Communities

Some of the best U.S. precedents for assisted living come from models within continuing-care retirement communities (CCRCs). Many of these were created to keep community residents out of skilled nursing for as long as possible. The rationale for promoting this additional element of the continuum of care has both financial and humane components. Individuals who move to CCRCs do so in part to plan for long-term care. When sponsored by a nonprofit entity, the financing system is a closed loop—the savings associated with reducing the number of individuals receiving nursing care can be used to lower initial endowments and monthly fees. Past research has generally supported this perspective. However, recent work by Newcomer and his colleagues (1992) revealed in one pilot study the tendency for assisted living to displace independent residents earlier. Clearly, more research must be initiated to study this phenomenon. Newcomer's work demonstrates how much discretionary authority the staff has in the placement decision, and how this can work either to keep residents out of nursing homes or to move them prematurely to a setting that is more efficient for the delivery of services.

The Medical and Residential Models of Assisted Living

Assisted living has developed two models of care, which can be described as medical and residential. The *residential* model physically separates assisted living and skilled nursing care units. In the residential model assisted living often involves separate residential pavilions having self-contained services or tethered to congregate housing. More intensive health services, such as physical and occupational therapy, are brought in when needed.

The **medical** model views assisted living as a health care environment, attaching it to or locating it within a nursing home. In this setting the term **personal care** is often used in place of assisted living. The medical model is influenced by its association with skilled nursing. As a wing of the health care center, the assisted living facility is often designed to be adapted to skilled care. As a floor of the nursing home, its placement above or below the skilled nursing floor establishes the width, depth, and overall configuration of each resident's room. In many medical model facilities the only difference between personal-care and skilled nursing units is that personal-care rooms have single occupancy and are carpeted. Often the same finishes, surfaces, and materials are specified. The medical model lessens the positive therapeutic benefit a residential environment can offer. Many medical-model facilities are so similar to nursing settings that it is hard for residents, visitors, and staff to distinguish them from institutional arrangements.

CCRCs throughout the country have embraced both models of assisted living. However, an alarming number of newly constructed for-profit and nonprofit sponsors have embraced the medical model. Because of its nursing home associations, this form of assisted living may cause continuing occupancy problems for its sponsors. The discovery of the potential advantages of the residential housing approach for the frail will, it is hoped, encourage a move toward creative residential models in the 1990s.

European Precedents

The northern European and English systems of long-term care utilize "sheltered care" housing arrangements for the frail that embrace homelike imagery in their design (Heumann and Boldy 1982; Weal and Weal 1988). European housing developments are smaller than their U.S. counterparts and

FIGURE 1.5. *Personal expression at the unit edge:* This sheltered housing project in England demonstrates how a variety of materials can enliven a double loaded corridor. Source: Hoglund, 1985.

have been designed and constructed as housing rather than as institutional environments.

Nursing homes in these countries are oriented to a medically indigent, subacute population and are far more residential in appearance. Materials whose use is restricted in the United States (e.g., wood, brick, and stone) are used inventively to establish a residential character. Furthermore, indirect artificial and natural lighting is often employed in corridors and social rooms, enhancing architectural expression and adding variety. The reliance on steel, concrete, and brick construction materials and a liberal attitude toward fire separations between public corridors and rooms have allowed Europeans to experiment more with overlapping spaces. Smaller areas are often carved out of bigger spaces, giving these facilities spatial interest.

Because these European cultures feel committed to producing humane, social environments for very old and frail people, they have experimented more formally with ideas about design and therapy. Recent projects involve the placement of small-scale group housing within age-integrated neighborhoods.

Experimental Assisted Living Projects

Powerful precedents for assisted living have also been provided by some well-publicized individual experiments conducted by state governments, nonprofit sponsors, and developers interested in pursuing alternatives to skilled nursing care. In Massachusetts during the late 1970s a collection of congregate homes was developed in conjunction with the Department of Elder Affairs and the Massachusetts Executive Office of Communities and Development (Welch et al. 1984). Of the twenty or so projects developed under this program the Captain Eldridge Congregate House received the most attention. Although it contains only eighteen units and is only slightly more sophisticated than a typical board-and-care facility, it provides an excellent example of how professionally managed, homelike settings can support the needs of the very old and frail. Some of the residents of the Captain Eldridge House came from nursing homes; others had been living alone in the community.

Oregon's Section 1915 Medicaid waiver experiment in assisted living affected thinking about such living arrangements throughout the United States. The residential environment along with the therapy and assessment program differentiated this housing alternative from the conventional nursing home. Medicaid waivers were used to fill the first experimental housing facilities, which moved residents from nursing homes into assisted living housing. The success of these early programs and their ability to deliver more humane and less expensive services to frail individuals quickly came to the attention of policymakers, encouraging expanded use of the program. Other states with recently implemented assisted living programs include Washington, New York, New Jersey, Florida, Maryland, Maine, Rhode Island, Connecticut, New Hampshire, and Massachusetts (Mollica et al. 1992; Lewin-ICF 1992; Kane and Wilson, 1993; Jenkins, 1992).

Sophisticated Board-and-care Homes

The development of assisted living facilities has also been affected by the increasing sophistication of board-and-care homes. These typically small-scale settings have been the traditional providers of services for the very old and frail (Hawes, Wildfire, and Lux 1993). Many have now achieved a higher degree of professional management while pursuing programs of a more sophisticated and therapeutic nature.

In addition, trade organizations and state associations have encouraged upgrading while aiding in the identification of substandard facilities. Board-and-care homes are small business enterprises that often have relatively short life spans. They have graduated from the "mom and pop" operations of years ago into entrepreneurial organizations seeking recognition and achievement as care providers by upgrading skills and developing a more enlightened approach to marketing (Adam 1993).

A professional association, the Assisted Living Facilities Association of America (ALFAA), was established in 1990 to represent the industry in Washington, D.C., to exchange information and provide peer associations, to promulgate industry standards, to educate the public, and to help providers address relevant issues that emerge in this industry. The American Association of Homes for the Aging (AAHA) has also created a working group within its organization to coordinate efforts and provide technical assistance to members about assisted living.

Service Overlay Concept

Assisted living is often used to describe a purpose-built housing type. However, it has also been conceptualized as a package of services that can be delivered to residents of independent or congregate housing arrangements and CCRCs. Critics of this *service overlay* approach believe it is limited and ineffective in serving those with the most critical needs, individuals who are confused or require frequent assistance. In many CCRCs or partial-continuum-of-care projects, assisted living is provided both as a service to residents in their units and as a dedicated facility for those who are most frail and impaired.

Outside of CCRCs the biggest boost for the service overlay concept has been through the federal assistance available from the Congregate Housing Services Program (CHSP). In 1990 CHSP served 2,000 people in thirty-three states living primarily in HUD-financed public housing. Personal-care services, as well as other medical and social services, are available for individuals with three or more ADL impairments. The success of this program in supporting very frail older people is not well documented, although it appears to have been effective from most accounts (Lewin-ICS 1992).

How Is Information About Assisted Living Recorded in the Formal Literature?

The emergence of the term *assisted living* to describe a specialized housing type and a philosophy of care is relatively new. The term does not appear in computer searches of formal literature until the mid-1980s. Trade publications such as *Contemporary Long-Term Care, Provider,* and *Retirement Housing Report* were among the first to use this term. The Long Term Care National Resource Center at UCLA/USC, when it developed an annotated bibliography (1990) on assisted living facilities, found it necessary to reference publications that use the terms **congregate housing, congregate house, board-and-care housing,** and **personal care** and could not rely solely on the term **assisted living**.

Several articles in the trade publication *Contemporary Long-Term Care* (CLTC) have dealt with the definition of *assisted living*. However, most of the articles published in this journal are professionally oriented rather than research based. In 1989 CLTC published the results of a survey ($n = 200$) distributed to readers of its magazine (Seip 1989c; Seip 1989b). The results sought to establish a basis of information about the nature of assisted living settings. A monograph, also produced from these data (Seip 1990b), explores more detailed aspects of the results of this survey.

Close scrutiny of the results reveals that the self-nomination process used to qualify respondents resulted in including a number of facilities that were either more institutional or less service intensive than "model" definitions of assisted living. For example, the data indicated that 33 percent of respondents had none or some of their units carpeted and that 30 percent had none or some of their units with private bathrooms. This indicates that as much as a third of the responding facilities appear to resemble institutions, without private access to toilets and/or carpet for floor covering. Furthermore, 20 to 25 percent of the facilities had less service-intensive programs than one would normally associate with a licensed facility. For example, 22 percent did not include assistance with dressing or bathing in their monthly fee. Only 59 percent provided toileting assistance within the monthly fee, and 26 percent did not include the services of a licensed nurse.

About half of the facilities surveyed, although they meet loosely established criteria, appear not to fit the model of assisted living environments described in this book. The problem of qualifying appropriate facilities indicates how elusive the definition of *assisted living* can be (Kalymun 1990) and how easily it can be merged with housing types on both sides of the care continuum.

A case study analysis conducted by Wilner (1988), based on seven exemplars, illustrates the range of management philosophies and project attributes that characterize the divergent directions being pursued in developing assisted living arrangements. Case study analysis, although narrow in its approach, is a useful method to define categories of alternatives. Welch, Parker, and Zeisel (1984), in their book *Independence Through Interdependence,* have defined basic attributes of small-scale housing and service arrangements.

The work of David Hoglund (1985) in classifying and categorizing a range of European examples of assisted living has also revealed how housing and services have been integrated with community centers in an effort to serve very old, frail people in European countries.

An evaluation of the Oregon assisted living and foster care programs by Rosalie Kane and her colleagues (1990) and a newer follow-up by Kane and Wilson (1993) have also provided clear indications of program strengths and weaknesses. Moreover, these documents comment on the promise associated with the continued refinement of the assisted living housing type (Kane 1993).

Broadening the search to include publications dealing with smaller board-and-care facilities reveals a much wider range of publication efforts. One major policy concern has been the regulation and classification of this housing type in various states (Hawes, Wildfire, and Lux 1993; U.S. House Subcommittee on Health and Long-Term Care 1989; Dobkin 1989; Benjamin and Newcomer 1986). Board-and-care housing has undergone scrutiny because smaller-scale arrangements licensed through state agencies and managed by individuals or families can include operations where bad practices and abuses go unnoticed.

Principles of Assisted Living Housing

In any model of assisted living it is important to recognize relationships between the social environment, the organizational context, and the physical environment. The social environment comprises friends and family; the organizational environment consists of the program's policies and staff; and the physical environment includes the unit within which the older resident lives and the common areas where programs operate.

Cohen and Weisman Therapeutic Goals

Cohen and Weisman (1991) have developed a model conceptualizing these relationships that is relevant for older frail people in assisted living arrangements. Their model, developed primarily for dementia facilities, is relevant to any context that seeks to foster care-giving and resident independence. Figure 1.6 suggests the interrelationships between social, organizational, and physical environments.

This model also implies that therapeutic goals shape, direct, and focus the interactions between these three components to meet the needs of a resident population. Cohen and Weisman have articulated nine therapeutic goals that underlie their work in dementia facilities:

1. Ensure safety and security.
2. Support functional ability through meaningful activity.
3. Heighten awareness and orientation.
4. Provide appropriate environmental stimulation and challenge.
5. Develop a positive social milieu.
6. Maximize autonomy and control.
7. Adapt to changing needs.
8. Establish links to the healthy and familiar.
9. Protect the need for privacy.

Calkin's Environmental and Behavior Issues

Calkin's (1988) book *Designing for Dementia* is oriented toward planning environments for the mentally impaired older person. It recognizes five en-

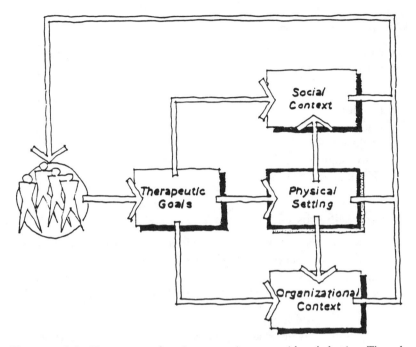

FIGURE 1.6. *Three types of environments impact resident behavior:* The relationship between residents, the physical environment, the social setting and facility policies and management is transactional. Source: Cohen and Weisman, 1991.

vironment and behavior issues that can be instrumental in creating a better fit among the person, his or her specific behaviors, and the environment. These five issues include the following:

Wayfinding and orientation
Privacy and socialization
Personalization
Safety and security
Competence in daily activities

Wilson's Six Components

Keren Brown Wilson (1990) recognizes six components that define her conceptualization of assisted living:

- Privacy
- Dignity
- Choice
- Independence
- Individuality
- Homelike surroundings.

Regnier and Pynoos's Environment and Behavior Issues

Regnier and Pynoos (1992) have identified a composite list of twelve environment-behavior principles. These principles combine and expand the preceding categories to identify a broad range of considerations for judging the responsiveness of the environment to the needs of very old frail people.

1. *Privacy.* Provide a place of seclusion, where a resident can be free from unauthorized intrusion.
2. *Social interaction.* Provide opportunities for social interaction and exchange.
3. *Control/choice/autonomy.* Promote opportunities for residents to make choices and to control events that influence outcomes.
4. *Orientation/wayfinding.* Foster a sense of orientation within the environment that reduces confusion and facilitates wayfinding.
5. *Safety/security.* Provide an environment that ensures each user will sustain no harm, injury, or undue risk.
6. *Accessibility and functioning.* Consider the ability to manipulate and access fixtures, appliances, cabinets, and environmental controls as the basic requirements for any functional environment.
7. *Stimulation/challenge.* Provide a stimulating environment that is also safe.
8. *Sensory aspects.* Changes in visual, auditory, and olfactory senses should be accounted for in the design of the environment.

9. *Familiarity.* Environments that use historical reference and solutions influenced by tradition can provide a sense of familiarity and continuity.
10. *Aesthetics/appearance.* Environments should be attractive, stimulating, and noninstitutional.
11. *Personalization.* Provide opportunities to make the environment personal and to mark it as the property of a single individual.
12. *Adaptability.* An adaptable or flexible environment can be made to fit changing personal characteristics.

A comprehensive model of assisted living should embrace these twelve principles and respond to the implications of each from both management and design perspectives. For example, the principle of privacy can be dealt with as either a management concept or a physical design solution. Training staff to knock before they enter a resident's room is just as important as placing a lock on the door. Management policies and environmental design must be coordinated to achieve privacy. In a double-occupancy arrangement where two unrelated individuals share a unit, eliciting courtesy and consid-

FIGURE 1.7. *A Dutch door, double hung window, and small "front porch" link each dwelling unit to a protected single loaded corridor:* The corridor leads units on two sides of a horseshoe shaped plan to shared spaces at the Annie Maxim House in Rochester, MA.

eration for one another is an important management issue, and making the physical environment conducive to sharing addresses the role of design. The response to the principle of privacy, like the eleven other principles listed, involves the physical arrangement of spaces as well as the management philosophy of the staff.

2. Developing the Project Concept

The term *assisted living* refers to both a philosophy of care and an idea about the character and appearance of the environment. To understand the range of possibilities the term implies it is important to isolate major attributes that, when combined, define models or concepts. Depending on how these are defined and combined, the building can range from a small, self-contained, stand-alone community dwelling to a large, multilevel, campus design. Chapter 1 advocates a residential model of long-term care using buildings that are approachable and that are not overwhelming. However, a range of models currently exists, and little evidence points to the desirability of pursuing only one approach. In general, most providers have sought to create buildings that house the smallest number of units that meet reasonable tests of service economy. Simply stated, the costs of service production should be low enough to gain reasonable economies of scale.

Form and Organization of Assisted Living Dwellings

The following five aspects appear to influence the form and organization of many assisted living dwellings: size, service autonomy, scale, building purpose, and appearance.

1. Size

The size of assisted living facilities can vary from less than five dwelling units to more than two hundred. A great deal of debate centers on the optimum number of units. Size requirements seem to vary in urban and rural contexts. Regulatory requirements also complicate the formula. In nursing homes, state regulation has become the basis for most size and configuration decisions. In assisted living, the smaller the number of residential units, the more difficult it is to provide in-depth twenty-four-hour care. In general, the smallest professionally managed and economically viable "stand-alone" models range from twenty to thirty units. Our analysis found major differences in the ways that the twenty-, forty-, and sixty-unit facilities were perceived and their "fit" within the neighborhood. A facility of more than eighty units takes on the appearance of an apartment building or hotel and requires a mid-rise scheme or substantially longer corridors to link units with common spaces.

2. Service Autonomy

Assisted living facilities can offer a full or partial continuum of care, or they can provide residents with only one level of care and "stand alone" in the community. In some facilities care is assessed on a case-managed basis, and residents living in the same dwelling differ considerably in their ability to function independently. Residents can also vary by type of disability. Some are confused mentally, whereas others are physically frail. Housing arrangements can be designed to separate these two resident groups or to "mainstream" them.

When it is linked to a full or partial continuum of care, assisted living can be made a part of the same building or can have its own separate identity. It can also be "linked" to independent housing, skilled nursing, or both in a project with a full continuum, like a CCRC.

Physically connecting assisted living with skilled nursing often results in a more institutional configuration. In such models assisted living is frequently conceptualized as a health care environment rather than as a housing environment with enriched services. Conversely, when physically linked to independent or congregate housing, assisted living is more likely to be perceived as a service-intensive residential setting.

Stand-alone facilities located in the community have no physical connection to either a nursing care or independent/congregate housing environment. These buildings, however, are often located near nursing or congregate facilities, to ease transfers to and from them.

3. Scale

The issue of building scale is important in defining the character and approachability of an assisted living environment. Facilities can consist of one, two, or three stories (low-rise); of four to nine stories (mid-rise); or of more than nine stories (high-rise). When assisted living units occur in a multistory building, they often occupy one or more self-contained floors. Low-rise models are the most prevalent, however, because site acquisition and construction costs are normally lower.

The issue of scale is often hotly debated in urban communities with few available sites. In these settings expensive land costs require more dwelling units to make a project economically feasible. When these buildings are out of scale with the surrounding building stock, neighbors may feel threatened. No study has measured the effect of new assisted living projects on the values of adjacent properties. However, the more residential a dwelling's appearance, the less threatening it will likely be to neighborhood residents.

A building can take on human scale by including references to elements common in residential housing. Some of these include porches, entry doors, residential-scale windows, and such materials as wood and brick. Scale is an issue often relative to the surrounding context and commonly established residential references.

4. Building Purpose

Another important factor is whether the building was originally designed as an assisted living facility or was remodeled from another use. Adaptive reuse projects have included former elementary schools, hospitals, hotels, nursing homes, and congregate/independent housing. One current trend involves the remodeling of wings or floors of congregate housing into assisted living.

Generally, purpose-built models should be centered around important behavioral design considerations. When they are designed this way, units can be arranged more efficiently and common spaces can be sized more precisely to fit needs. However, older buildings often contain charming qualities and unique features that make them memorable and interesting. Older houses in particular make interesting subjects for adaptive reuse. Adaptively reused institutional facilities like hospitals and nursing homes, on the other hand, offer major challenges. The nature of the original design can often compromise function, and its institutional appearance can seem stark and unappealing.

5. Appearance

The appearance of assisted living buildings depends in part on the building precedents from which their imagery is borrowed. Facilities can take direc-

FIGURE 2.1. *The front porch, steeply sloping roof, overhang details and complex massing configuration are residential in character:* Elder-Homestead in Minnetonka, MN was inspired by the 19th c. vernacular Minnesota farmhouse.

tion and form from a range of housing and hospitality environments. Some of the most desirable precedents include the large mansion house and the compact European-style bed-and-breakfast hotel. Assisted living environments that borrow their imagery from transformations of the house are often designed as villas or country homes. Their overall size and scale may give them the appearance of an apartment dwelling, but the portion of the development that contains common spaces is derived from the house. The compact hotel is defined by spacious common facilities linked to a residential massing configuration of three to six stories. The building's style can also provide important cues about how the building fits into both the surrounding neighborhood and the region. Residential expressions can vary from one region to another. The building should appear related to housing and should not create ambiguity about its character. Commercial materials, details, and treatments can confuse residents, family members, and staff, who are trying to comprehend what kind of building this is by noting the exterior and interior details of the setting.

The preceding five attributes, used in various combinations, define a range of assisted living housing concepts. The applications—in terms of image, scale, and residential reference—are amazingly varied. However, the major challenge in developing an attractive and viable facility is achieving a compelling residential character while satisfying the economies of scale necessary to deliver a range of personal-care services cost-effectively. A successful project concept can be measured by how effectively it achieves the two competing goals of residential appearance and service cost efficiency.

Spatial Zones

Another way of conceptualizing the design of an assisted living setting is to think about the territorial zones associated with a building's site and internal organization. These include outdoor and indoor spaces and vary from highly public to highly private spaces. Each zone exists as a separate typology but is affected by its co-existence with other zones. The following defines five major indoor and outdoor zones or territories. A project's design must recognize the possibilities for integration of zones and the need to respect the integrity of each zone. These five zones include the following: peripheral outdoor spaces, shared and private outdoor places, common shared spaces, service facilities and resident units.

Peripheral Outdoor Spaces

The periphery around the building includes the parking lot; front yard, side yard, and rear yard setbacks; and the site edge. This can be conceptualized as the outer "donut" between the building and the property line.

Shared and Private Outdoor Places

If the building form does not define outdoor spaces, they may be defined by fences, hedges, or pavement. Many projects seek to define outdoor spaces in the form of a courtyard, porch, or patio. Shared outdoor spaces can be used actively or passively. In facilities that cater to Alzheimer's victims, contained outdoor areas can be used during pleasant weather for residents who desire to walk or exercise. Courtyard areas that provide controlled views can extend indoor activities outdoors, thus expanding their utility and attractiveness.

Common Shared Spaces

Common spaces include rooms shared by residents, staff, and visitors. They typically range from very public areas (e.g., the entry lobby) to semi-

FIGURE 2.2. *The massing and design of buildings can be inspired by neighboring structures:* The roof slope, gable ends and balcony rails of this service house in Denmark were designed to fit a neighborhood design vocabulary.

public spaces (e.g., the living room) and semiprivate spaces (e.g., an exercise or therapy space). In most facilities common rooms are clustered in one location, often adjacent to the entry or administrative offices. Frequently, however, decentralized social lounges are employed throughout the facility to serve clusters of six to eight units.

Unit clusters facilitate friendship formation and informal helping exchanges. Specific activity spaces, such as an exercise room or multipurpose room, can also be located in another area of the building.

Service Facilities

Service facilities typically involve "back-of-the-house" spaces for staff, including facilities for food production, housekeeping, and administration.

Resident Units

Typical resident units are either single-occupied studio or one-bedroom units. However, in facilities designed for low-income residents, designs often accommodate two unrelated individuals sharing a unit. Newer assisted living facilities designed for higher-income recipients may include larger one-bedroom/den or even two-bedroom suites. Regardless of income, units should contain an area for food storage and preparation. This is important from the perspectives of both function and self-concept, because it defines the image of a "complete" residential unit. The bathroom should be accessible to older people confined to a wheelchair and to those who may need assistance in bathing or toileting.

Planning and Design Directives

The introductory chapter concluded with twelve broad environment and behavior principles. These define general goals that form the basis of a philosophy of physical design intervention and program management.

The following ten planning and design directives are more specific in their orientation. They establish a position for design intervention that suggests that specific priorities be the focus of design action. In this sense they are like objectives that complement and extend environmental-behavior principles. They include

1. Residential character and image.
2. Function, behavioral purpose, and variety.
3. Outdoor areas defined as rooms.
4. Support for family interactions.
5. Adaptive environments.
6. Public to private continuum of spaces.
7. Sensory stimulation.
8. Indoor/outdoor connections.
9. Community exchanges.
10. Activity generators that instill vitality.

These directives should be used to advocate a better fit between the needs of assisted living residents and the design opportunities presented by the environment.

1. Residential Character and Image

One of the most powerful impacts the physical environment can have is to establish behavioral expectations based on the character, image, and appearance of a setting. The way a building is understood through past perceptions of similar building types establishes expectations for performance and future behavior. For example, visiting a hospital comes with a collection of

FIGURE 2.3. *Desirable housing stock can be remodeled or adaptively reused from existing housing stock:* The John Bertram House in Salem, MA was remodeled and expanded to meet contemporary standards.

feelings and assumptions based on past experience. This is validated as a person enters and experiences the place. The mid-rise form; the wide, double-loaded (i.e., having rooms on two sides) corridor configurations; the nurses' station locations; the uniformed personnel; and the entry designed for emergency vehicles all reinforce ideas about the identity of the place. The more typical these responses are, the more they become internalized. We anticipate certain aspects and behave according to pre-established norms.

Nursing homes in our society are designed around a hospital model. They appear efficient, clean, and clinical and are designed as places to convalesce rather than as places to live. In reality, nursing homes are a hybrid setting but frequently function more as a home to older residents than as a hospital environment. When character and imagery center on the appearance of an institution and an institutional life-style, residents, staff, and family members are more likely to view older people as sickly rather than as just old and frail. The appearance of the environment thus affects our assumptions and feelings about these places and the people who live in them.

The building should appear residential, not institutional, and should reflect the history and culture of the region. This appearance should not be achieved through a façade that is tacked onto the front of a nursing home reminiscent of cape cod or Spanish revival. It should represent a genuine investigation into the historic nature of residential forms in the region. Vernacular housing details, which characterize aspects of the pre–World War II housing stock, should be inspected. The scale and organization of rooms should fit a residential model. Furthermore, residential materials and details common to the regional housing stock should be scrutinized for meaning and fit. In one part of the country this might mean that a craftsman-style porch enclosure would be appropriate. In another, brick, stucco, or wood might be more familiar. The specification of doors, windows, floor materials, ceiling treatments, and wall coverings should be sensitive to the concern of developing imagery that is consistent with a residential character. At stake is not just the "feel-good" appearance of the setting, but its influence on how people behave within that context.

2. Function, Behavioral Purpose, and Variety

When Vitruvius (Morgan 1960) used the terms *commodity, firmness,* and *delight* to describe the basic tenets of architecture, he recognized the obligation of architecture to respond to a city, a building, or an individual room. In housing for special users who are mentally or physically disabled, the need to examine how function is met is very important. These individuals are often at risk with regard to the environment. Small impediments that a younger person can overcome may be difficult for an older frail person. Thus freedom and ability to access the environment are regulated by the design of the setting.

Each common space should have a clear behavioral purpose and function. Designers should understand, anticipate, and hypothesize expected behaviors that can be encouraged and supported within each designated

FIGURE 2.4. *The rosewood room is a formal and dignified parlor:* Located near
the entry of Rosewood Estate, in Roseville, MN it provides a place for residents to
entertain family members and friends.

common space. Rehearsing activities and imagining how they are to be carried out in different ways at different times of the day and night, on week-
ends and weekdays, and during the summer or winter helps one imagine
how well the room supports or limits activity. A variety of spaces should be
available for a range of social, intellectual, and recreational activities. Some
common spaces should be formal; others should be more informal.

Each space should elicit a range of behaviors that conform to the formal
and informal expectations associated with different rooms. Thus spaces are
likely to be proportioned differently. They can elicit different responses and
can appear quite different from one another, even though they share the
same corridor or are adjacent to one another. Card playing, dancing, conversation, and crafts activities require different light levels, acoustic liveliness, furniture, equipment, floor, and wall treatments. It is the constellation
of activities, materials, and furnishings that make spaces unique and prompt
residents to pursue different behaviors within each setting.

Each room should be shaped, sized, and proportioned to provide focus
and organization for the furniture and activities envisioned within that
space. Rooms should also be flexible enough to accommodate different use

patterns as needs for new activities and services emerge. A full range of spatial linkages and connections should be employed, allowing rooms and activities to overlap with edges that can be visually or sonically penetrated.

The development of a "user's manual" for the project is a good idea. This can alert management and service personnel to the original intentions associated with each room. Although spaces may not always conform to an early theory, knowing the specific ideas around which the space was designed can facilitate adjustments as the project matures or can provide effective feedback for the design of a similar space in a new building.

3. Outdoor Areas Defined as Rooms

The configuration of the building can greatly contribute to the definition of outdoor areas. Buildings that form courtyards define outdoor rooms. Buildings that are placed in the center of a landscape often depend on trees, shrubs, garden walls, planter beds, and hedges to define outdoor spaces. All buildings, be they simple objects or complex configurations, have a relationship with the landscape.

This relationship can be developed through the entry sequence, a visual connection between indoor and outdoor spaces, outdoor terrace extensions, or landscape materials that define edges. It is important to remember that trees, plant materials, and garden walls are to the outside of a building as walls and built-in furniture are to its inside. They should be used to give outdoor space definition and distinction. Older people often prefer to sit around the edges of these spaces rather than the center. Thus furniture placements that are "closely coupled" to interior corridors, common rooms, and exit doors are often the most popular (Regnier 1985; Carstens 1990).

One of the most important opportunities that outdoor spaces provide is the ability to extend views and activities from indoors to outdoors. Many well-known architects, such as Frank Lloyd Wright and Rudolph Schindler, were admired for their ability to create landscapes that extend the perception of space into adjacent garden areas. Rooms that successfully do this are perceived as light, airy, and exhilarating. Gardens can support private meditation or highly social activities. Typically, living rooms, dining rooms, craft rooms, and exercise spaces can be extended outdoors for a range of uses. Outdoor spaces can also provide rich settings for sensory stimulation. Colors, smells, sounds, the activities of birds and animals, and the stimulation of fresh air and sunlight can make outdoor settings highly evocative.

4. Support for Family Interactions

Maintaining affective ties with family members is one of the most important objectives an assisted living residence can achieve. Many believe that family interactions occur irrespective of environmental influence. However, family members can be alienated by a building's appearance, its lack of friendliness, and its inability to accommodate personal exchanges with residents. The building should therefore provide places that invite and support a range of family interactions. When these spaces facilitate or overlook activities, family members can find things to do that structure their interaction, making it stimulating for both residents and their visitors. Administrative policies should encourage and involve family members in the daily lives of residents.

Because family members often take residents out of the building to visit the doctor or a neighborhood restaurant, it should be relatively easy to move residents in and out of the building. The design of the entry should facilitate transfer to and from an automobile. Outdoor spaces, gardens, and porches can provide destinations to visit that are novel and enhance interaction.

FIGURE 2.5. *Fire stairs in European housing are often glass enclosed spaces that allow daylight to enter the center of the bulding while encouraging residents to walk between floors:* The stair at De Overloop in Almere-Haven, Netherlands also has a controlled view of a beautiful garden pool.

The resident's unit is also an important setting for family interaction. When a unit is occupied by only one person and has space for food storage and preparation, a private bathroom, and enough area to accommodate an overnight stay, family relationships can be enhanced.

5. Adaptive Environments

An environment that adapts to the changing needs of residents can maximize independence. The building and the service program should be designed to change as residents age in the facility. The environment should be both "prosthetic" and "therapeutic," working toward the maintenance of existing competencies and the restoration of lost abilities. Thus it should assist residents to overcome their lost abilities but continue to challenge them. This sometimes involves placing an individual in a managed-risk situation where the environment is challenging. For example, walking to the dining room without assistance builds competence but raises the possibility of injury by slipping or falling. Good clinical judgments should balance risk and challenge for each resident.

In the dwelling unit the bathroom and kitchen are the key spaces where adaptive changes should be considered. Here residents must often carry out activities of daily living that become more difficult with age. Safety in these two rooms is of prime importance. Grab bars, shower stalls, easily manipulated fixtures, and easily reached storage areas can make these settings useful for a longer period of time as an older person becomes less independent and unable to carry out a full range of activities by themselves.

Increasing the amount of assisted personal care also presumes that key spaces like the bathroom are large enough to facilitate assistance. The space adjacent to the toilet and around the shower should be great enough to account for an additional person who may be needed to help the older resident.

6. Public-to-Private Continuum of Spaces

Balancing the location, relationship, size, and number of activity areas with spaces that support privacy is an important design issue. Most housing accommodates a continuum of public to private spaces from the front lobby to the resident's bathroom. In an assisted living setting four spatial typologies define this continuum. The most accessible is public space, such as the front porch or entry lobby, where residents and visitors are welcome. Semipublic spaces form the next layer. These are typically spaces that outsiders are invited to share, such as a parlor, dining room, or living room. Semiprivate spaces are normally shared by a small number of residents and can include a decentralized lounge or living room space near a cluster of units. Finally, the dwelling unit and most particularly the bedroom and bathroom provide areas for the greatest privacy and intimacy.

One of the stark contrasts between a nursing facility and a well-designed assisted living environment is the nursing home's lack of a clearly developed public-to-private continuum. Corridors are semipublic and resident rooms are unlocked and open, often exposing residents to the scrutiny of strangers. At night, noise generated by staff and residents with sleep disturbances permeates the facility, making it difficult to achieve an uninterrupted evening of sleep.

Public spaces should encourage interactions among residents, family, staff, and visitors. Semipublic spaces should be designed to encourage chance encounters, social exchange, informal conversations, and small group interactions. Spaces within the facility should reflect a homelike environment that balances the desire for social interaction with that for privacy.

7. Sensory Stimulation

As we age we lose our ability to process a range of sensory inputs vividly. Colors are muted, tastes and smells are fainter, and hearing loss accumulates. The building and the activities it contains, along with outdoor spaces, should be designed to stimulate residents in a variety of ways. Losses in hearing, sight, touch, smell, and taste should be recognized and accommodated through pleasurable experiences that reinforce and stimulate the senses. For example, floral fragrances and familiar smells like that of food cooking should permeate the setting in a way that provides a reminder of home. The specification of artificial and enhanced natural light especially for task-related circumstances should compensate for age-related losses in visual acuity. The sonic environment should minimize unneeded, unwanted background noise, making it easy for residents to communicate with one another.

Multiple cues can alert residents who have lost their ability to see or hear. Elevators that use a tone and light capitalize on multiple cuing. It is also important to be aware of the stereotypic smells, sounds, and lack of positive stimulation that characterize the nursing home. In these settings residents are often exposed to a very narrow range of enhanced sensory stimulation, which can lead to boredom and depression.

Outdoor environments provide a rich array of sensory stimulation because they contain textures, colors, activities, scents, sounds, and micro-

FIGURE 2.6. *Gardens stimulate the senses:* Fragrant jasmine at the Jewish Home for the Aged in Reseda, California is planted in raised beds which residents who are seated or in wheelchairs can enjoy.

climatic differences. Allowing residents to sense this vast array of experiences is an easy way to increase opportunities for enhanced sensory stimulation.

8. Indoor-Outdoor Connections

One of the greatest sources of stimulation for persons with difficulty in ambulation is to sit on a porch or patio and view activities taking place on the perimeter of the site. During inclement weather, window seats, attached greenhouse enclosures, bay windows, and winter gardens located near the edge of the building allow residents the protection of a conditioned space with a view toward the activity of the outdoor world.

Two types of space can be defined at the edge of buildings between indoors and outdoors. The first includes indoor spaces like the greenhouse or bay window mentioned earlier. These spaces allow residents to view the outdoors from a protected setting. The second typology of outdoor-indoor space includes porches and arcades. These provide limited protection against sun and wind but also allow residents to perceive the full range of sensory aspects associated with the outside world. The "closely coupled" linkage of these outdoor spaces with interior spaces provides additional security, which is often important for the older resident with ambulatory difficulties. In many cases residents with profound limitations substitute this exposure to the outside world for more direct engagement like walking around the neighborhood.

Relationships and linkages between indoors and outdoors should be pursued wherever opportunities exist. Viewing attractively landscaped outdoor areas from shared spaces or from individual dwelling units can be a source of stimulation and pleasure.

In Frost Belt locations, plant materials located indoors within a conservatory, greenhouse, or atrium, can imbue a space with special meaning. Indoor and outdoor landscaping should reinforce an appreciation of natural ecology. Off-site views of people, birds, traffic, butterflies, and squirrels also capture the activity and complexity of urban or suburban life. This allows residents to be passive observers and to experience these activities vicariously by watching others. Porches and balconies that create protected outdoor spaces often have important historic significance to residents. Many have used these features during their lifetime and their presence invites continuity by nurturing and accommodating pleasant past experiences.

9. Community Exchanges

Institutions are often located in areas that discourage relationships with the surrounding neighborhood. Traditionally, prisons, asylums, and hospitals have been located either away from population centers or near commercial areas. Nursing homes suffer by association with these other institutional land uses. This often results in an isolated existence with few linkages and connections to the surrounding community or.neighborhood. Assisted living residences should respond to this segregated pattern of land use classification by seeking new forms of integration.

FIGURE 2.7. *The erker is a European square bay window that overhangs the street:* It allows residents to view activity up and down the street from a cozy alcove at the edge of the unit.

Facilities and services should be designed and programmed to compensate for isolation. Programs such as on-site child care or adult day care can create important relationships between the facility and the community. These programs provide ways for the facility to be a more vital and effective community resource.

Community integration can be pursued in three fundamental ways. The first is through programs and services offered at the site that cater to neighborhood residents. These are most likely to be older people living in the surrounding community who have therapeutic or social needs that an assisted living residence can satisfy. Other groups can also be attracted, such as children, whose needs for nurturing and stimulation are complementary. The second way to create more effective integration is to manufacture services (e.g., meals on wheels, homemaker, home care, and electronic emergency communications) that serve the older neighborhood population in their own home. This makes the facility a community service provider rather than a static single-purpose institution. Thirdly, older residents can be encouraged to leave the facility through mini-bus and family-escorted trips to familiar neighborhood locations, such as the bank, beauty shop, or church or synagogue. Facilitating these important community connections keeps the older person in touch with life outside the housing project.

10. Activity Generators That Instill Vitality

In contrast to living an isolated life with home-delivered services in the community, assisted living provides residents with the opportunity to establish meaningful and satisfying social relationships with other people. The ability to create new friends and confide in others is a powerful influence that can mitigate depression and significantly enhance quality of life. Depending on how a building is designed and management is trained, the environment can be friendly or alienating. One important ingredient that greatly affects informal social encounters is the placement of common rooms in locations of predictable pedestrian traffic flows.

Such spaces as the dining room, entry, and residents' mailbox area are traffic generators that should be used strategically to create, animate, and define areas within the facility that residents find interesting to visit. The use of some rooms—including informal lounges, a library, an information center, or a hospitality area—is greatly affected by casual pedestrian traffic. Such areas as assembly rooms, a beauty/barber shop, or health clinic are organized around scheduled events or appointments. These spaces do not benefit from close association with traffic generators.

Predictable circulation routes, such as the pathway that connects the elevator to the front door, can influence the popularity of various rooms and must be used to clear advantage (Howell 1980). It is also important that residents be able to "preview" spaces before they enter them and feel comfortable with their social dynamics. Living in an assisted living situation is like being in a sorority, fraternity, or dormitory. Most of the residents' social contact will be limited to others living there. Design features should be sensitive to the fact that not everyone will seek one another's friendship. Previewing a space before entering allows residents control over social encoun-

FIGURE 2.8. *Living room spaces at Sunrise are scaled to accommodate furniture conversation groupings:* Their adjacency to a cluster of 5 to 7 resident rooms provides easy access for small group activities.

ters. Finally, unit entries clustered together or around small living rooms can foster informal friendships that may lead to helping relationships.

Conclusions

Although the preceding ten directives somewhat narrow the application of principles introduced in the first chapter, they provide detail, direction, and spirit to the design of assisted living housing. They should be considered in the design and layout of spaces as well as in the development of the overall building concept. Many of these directives influence how the site can be interpreted and how common rooms on the first floor are organized. They also provide practical suggestions about how the building and common spaces function to meet the needs of residents now and as they age in the facility.

Developing a creative building concept involves establishing the size, scale, orientation, appearance, and management approach to the project. The concept should be sensitive to the larger community context and specific to the physical parameters of the site. The chapters that follow will provide more specific advice about how design considerations, management philosophy, and the financing strategy affect concept development.

3. Designing the Physical Environment

This chapter addresses issues of design as they relate to the physical environment. Although this is often accomplished in conjunction with a management plan and a financing approach, the innovations presented here are purposefully segregated from these other influences. The chapter is divided into thirteen topic areas that address issues raised by the 130 submissions provided by participants. Examples were inspected for face value and then investigated further to identify the underlying idea. In many cases the general concept was more powerful than the specific example cited. After identifying larger ideas, specific examples were assembled as illustrations. In assembling categories many submitted ideas were considered timid but tangible examples that illustrated the topic and demonstrated how each idea could be implemented.

Topics are given so they can be scrutinized further. Most examples are best adapted rather than copied, because they can be refined through specific application. The ideas presented are by no means exhaustive and in some cases are inconsistent. We believe the topics have value in stimulating the imagination and that the examples cited increase confidence in the utility and feasibility of the basic concepts. We hope this chapter will be used to reinvent and expand the suggestions listed.

Design Innovation and Exploration

Each of the thirteen topics is introduced by a statement that defines its importance as an "area of innovation" and its associated potential for facility improvement. Topics range in scale and magnitude from items associated with the design of the unit to planning concepts that involve mixing different land uses. Examples are presented in an effort to describe the range of possible applications. The thirteen areas are the following:

1. Dwelling unit features.
2. Neighborhood unit clusters.
3. Creative use of natural light.
4. Use of spatial hierarchy.
5. Site design considerations.
6. Therapy and architectural design.
7. Residential materials, surfaces, and finishes.
8. Exterior design considerations.
9. Visitation for the family.
10. Codes and regulations.
11. Common, recreational, and social spaces.
12. Corridors and connecting spaces.
13. Linkages to the community.

1. Dwelling Unit Features

The dwelling unit offers the greatest opportunity for privacy. How privacy is assured has been an area that has differentiated skilled nursing from assisted living. In assisted living, access to a single-occupied, lockable dwelling unit is generally assumed. In the typical nursing home the majority of units are doubled-occupied.

In addition to providing greater privacy and control over the environment, successful assisted living facilities offer many other dwelling unit features oriented toward an independent life-style.

Kitchen. One controversial issue is that of food preparation within the unit and the corresponding presence of a "kitchen." In some facilities a strip kitchenette located against a wall with a sink, refrigerator, and stove top is considered standard, although regulations concerned with food storage and safety may limit the size and completeness of the kitchen. The presence of a stove top, however, is controversial. If a resident's ability to use this appliance safely is in question, it should be easy to disconnect. Providers who feel kitchens are unnecessary believe that they reduce usable space in the unit by introducing a feature that is rarely used. The counterargument is that a kitchen can stimulate a range of independent behaviors that provide therapeutic targets for building competency.

FIGURE 3.1. *The character of dwelling units are transformed when older residents bring their own furniture:* In this project, residents brought light fixtures and throw rugs, as well as furniture.

Storage. Well-designed units provide storage in the bathroom and near the bedroom. Typically, decentralized storage located where items are needed is the most useful and efficient arrangement. Storage areas should be considered for personal hygiene items in the bathroom, towels and bed linens, food and kitchen utensils, and clothing; space should also be available for games and writing and hobby materials. Better-designed units anticipate resident use patterns by building accessible, easy-to-manipulate storage in a range of appropriate places.

In the Aldersgate Village project in Topeka, Kansas, movable wardrobe closets have been utilized to augment existing storage. These portable units appear as furniture pieces and can be moved within each unit to the best location.

Grasp and Manipulation. Designing for physiological changes often involves making an environment easier to manage. Kitchen and bathroom fixtures should be specified that are easy for arthritic hands to manipulate. Door hardware should be lever style and pulls for cabinetry and storage spaces should be looped for easy grasp. Window hardware should be easy to unlock and the window simple to open. Oversized heating, ventilating, and air-conditioning (HVAC) controls that are easy to read and special safety items like antiscald devices in bathroom showers are also important.

Regulations used to specify furniture in institutional environments can limit residents from bringing their own furniture. Institutional furniture items such as a hospital-style adjustable bed or an over-the-bed tray are still mistakenly required by regulations in some states.

Bathrooms. The issue of handicapped accessibility is somewhat controversial. Many sponsors recognize the need to design units so that patients confined to a wheelchair and helpers assisting in transfers have adequate room. However, another competing philosophy involves making the scale of bathrooms more intimate so that an older frail person can navigate by leaning on the edges of counters, grasping doorknobs, or using towel racks for support. To accommodate this the John Bertram House in Salem, Massachusetts, has specified 1-inch-diameter grab bars as towel racks, presuming the extra strength and the more secure connection to the wall may be used by residents for support. One approach gaining popularity involves designing the bathroom so that it meets wheelchair-turning requirements and then supplying it with storage cabinets and ledges to create a more intimate context for the ambulatory frail older resident. If wheelchair access is necessary, storage units and ledges can be removed. Approaches like this recognize the range of capabilities and the changing physical condition of residents as they age.

Most assisted living housing specifies showers within each unit with enough space in the bathroom to accommodate attendants who provide assistance to the wheelchair-bound or the very frail. In most settings a bathtub or whirlpool option is available to residents in a special supervised room where a commercial tub outfitted with a lift is provided. Some controversy exists over bathing facilities. Sponsors with showers in each unit designed

FIGURE 3.2. *The "Bistro" at Sunrise in Falls River, MD is open to the community:* It provides a place for family members to go and hosts neighbors from the church next door on Sunday afternoons.

to be used with assistance claim bathing in the privacy of the unit preserves the sanctity of this activity. Advocates for supervised whirlpool baths conducted in a separate room set aside for this purpose view bathing as a pleasurable and hygienic experience. They believe residents enjoy the stimulation and therapy that results from a whirlpool bath. Both bathing philosophies have strong advocates and are not mutually exclusive.

Making the unit adaptable to the changing needs of the older person is a principle that can be implemented by adjusting the level of service and adapting the unit to increase safety and supportiveness.

Unit Size. A major difference between older and newer assisted living developments and those targeted toward middle- to upper-income residents is the size and number of larger one- or two-bedroom units. The specification of larger units parallels a trend in congregate living arrangements, symbolizing the desire on the part of older residents to maximize choice, increase autonomy, and maintain control over their environment. Small dwelling units of less than 300 square feet often resemble skilled nursing rooms rather than an independent apartment. The need for more space for family guests or a private-duty nurse has also increased the popularity of larger units. Clearly, the cost of the unit is affected by an increase in size and can only be considered when facilities can recover this expense in the form of higher rents or deeper subsidies.

Other Features. Other popular features receiving increasing interest are first-floor patios and upper-floor balconies. These provide variety to the housing facade while introducing a place for plants and an area to sit outside near the privacy of the dwelling unit. In some states ground-floor egress requirements for nonambulatory residents have mandated swing or sliding doors from the unit to outdoors.

Maximizing daylight in units is a another important consideration. Specifying 8-foot window heights or units that are narrower in depth (exterior wall to corridor wall) increases the amount of daylight reaching interior spaces. Another considerate feature is the specification of lower sill heights, which allows residents to view outside activities from the bed or from an easy chair.

Many of these features are not unique to housing for the elderly. In fact, many are well documented in guidelines that advocate considerate design for older people in independent, purpose-built housing (AIA Foundation 1985; Green et al. 1975; Lawton 1975; Zeisel, Epp, and Demos 1977). What is new is the application of these principles to the design of dwelling units for very old frail people, since many existing personal-care units have been designed around a medical model that resembles intermediate nursing care rather than a residential dwelling unit.

2. Neighborhood Unit Clusters

The desire to create a manageable intimate residential scale in assisted living housing has encouraged various approaches to clustering units often referred to as "neighborhoods." The philosophy behind this approach is twofold. Unit clusters foster informal friendships and helping networks between neighbors. Moreover, the physical envelope that accommodates these clusters can lead to a more articulated, complex building form, reducing the monolithic appearance of a project from the street.

Interest in a more intimate unit of physical and social organization is a response to the long, double-loaded corridors of skilled nursing facilities. The typical nursing home wing takes its organizational form from the distance requirements (room portal to nurses station) specified in regulatory codes.

The desire to create a scale of unit organization that encourages informal social interaction has led to a range of different solutions. The optimum number of units within a cluster normally falls between six and ten, large enough to form a critical mass and to provide residents with a choice of neighbors. In developments of less than twenty units, clustering is less important. Floor separations and the location of shared space in buildings of this size create natural divisions that reduce perceived scale.

Unit cluster organizations are being applied more frequently to nursing home environments (AIA 1992). Decentralized nurses' desks are being used in conjunction with smaller activity/dining rooms that service ten to fifteen residents. This rethinking is based on how care and supervision can be more personally and effectively provided.

Unit Clusters. At Elder-Homestead in Minnetonka, Minnesota, four residential units are placed around a shared living room called a cluster parlor. In this plan each residential unit consists of a bedroom/living room, bathroom, and kitchen. To create a more intimate linkage between the residential unit and cluster parlor, Dutch doors and double-hung windows were installed. To avoid stringent fire code restrictions, each four-unit cluster was treated as a single shared living unit. Fire wall separations occur between the cluster parlor and a corridor that leads to a single shared dining room.

Fox Acres, in Memphis, Tennessee, has pursued a unique physical configuration by clustering six cottages (each of which accommodates four residents) around a shared common space. The total development of 120 units consists of five of these twenty-four-unit clusters. The resident unit, called a suite, includes a bedroom and a bathroom. A group of four suites—clustered around a shared kitchenette, dining alcove, tub room, and living room—is referred to as a cottage. Six cottages (twenty-four suites) surround two lounge areas, two group dining areas, an administrative desk, a laundry, and a serving kitchen. Meals prepared in a central kitchen are transported to each twenty-four-suite cluster.

Another common approach to clustering involves placing units around a shared lounge or informal meeting place. This approach is used in Borden Court, an assisted living facility in Bloomington Hills, Michigan. Here a Y-shaped space created by joining two corridors provides an informal sitting area for residents and space for an administrative desk. Nursing personnel outposted here keep tabs on residents. A small dining room adjacent to

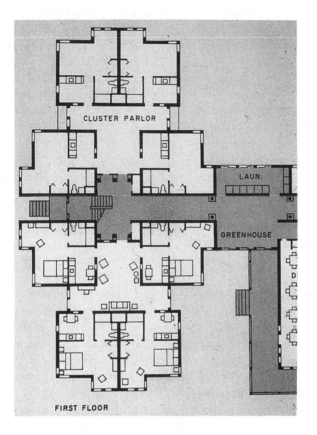

FIGURE 3.3. *Four units are clustered around a common parlor:* At Elder-Homestead parlors serve as shared social spaces. Units are linked to parlors through Dutch doors and double hung windows.

the lounge allows residents living in this unit cluster to eat their meals nearby. The decentralized lounge and dining room reduces travel distance for residents and minimizes the staff time required to move wheelchair-bound residents from their unit to the dining area.

The concept of developing family-style unit clusters around self-contained dining and lounge spaces has been utilized in a number of assisted living facilities designed for Alzheimer's victims. A good example of this concept carried out at a residential scale is Woodside Place in Oakmont, Pennsylvania (see chapter 6). In this plan three small, cottagelike pavilions are interconnected by corridors. The dining room and living room of each cottage are linked to a corridor that connects each unit to several special-purpose common rooms where informal and organized activities are available. The corridor serves as a passive diversion for residents who watch the activity along it and as a wandering pathway for more restless residents.

At Rosewood Estate in Roseville, Minnesota, sixty-eight units have been organized around eighteen lounge spaces in a design that devotes nearly half its gross floor area to common space (see chapter 6). The building is organized in three segments. A one-story grade change from the front to the back of the site allows the three-story building to appear as two stories from the street. The center portion of the building has the appearance of a large colonial house, whereas the eight units clustered on each floor at the two ends of the building create "social cul-de-sacs" for residents living there.

Building Clusters. Another approach to unit organization has been to limit the overall scale to that of a single-family house. In Mesa, Arizona, Senior Housing and Management Group has experimented with the idea of grouping six conventionally sized houses on both sides of a residential street. Each home accommodates ten residents and is designed to appear as a normal single-family dwelling. A central kitchen in one of the houses prepares food that is delivered to warm-up kitchens in each adjoining house. Placing the units adjacent to one another allows for economies of scale in service delivery while maintaining a scale that is consistent with the surrounding neighborhood.

Sunrise Retirement Homes and Communities uses a similar strategy in its Bluemont Park development in Arlington, Virginia. Instead of creating a single large 150-unit building on the site, it constructed three separate fifty-unit buildings. Each contains a dining room as well as social and recreational spaces. The buildings, situated on a steep hillside, connect at the lower-floor level. The kitchen, laundry, and heating/cooling plant are centralized and serve each building through a below-grade service corridor. Two of the buildings house slightly more independent residents; the third is for more frail residents. Each building has its own identity and configuration established by site conditions and off-site views. Choosing to develop the project as a three-building complex minimized financial risk and allowed phasing.

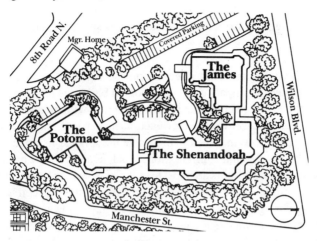

FIGURE 3.4. *Three inter-connected but separate buildings reduce the perceived size of this complex:* Three buildings at the Bluemont Park Sunrise in Maryland, each have 50 units. A lower level corridor links all three together allowing food and care services to be conveniently distributed.

In both these examples reductions in the scale of the building lessened the overall impact on the surrounding neighborhood.

3. Creative Use of Natural Light

The use of natural light in architecture is a profound and powerful design element. The color, intensity, and quality of natural light are difficult, if not impossible, to achieve with artificial sources. Natural light typically enters a building through windows and skylights. Tall windows oriented toward the south and the east provide the best opportunity for bringing daylight into interior spaces. Sunlight from windows oriented to the west is more direct and harder to control, especially in the late afternoon. Natural light from the north is reflected and is more subtle. It is a favorite for artists' studios. In Frost Belt locations, however, windows that face north can be a source of cold drafts through infiltration or convection.

The amount of light entering a building through a window is generally a function of the size and height of the window, its cardinal orientation, the season, and any building or landscape impediments that could block it. Interior spaces located further than 25 to 30 feet from a window require supplemental lighting from artificial sources or skylights mounted on the roof.

Skylights. Skylights are only effective on the upper floor of multistory buildings. To have an impact on lower floors in buildings of more than one story, skylights must be constructed in conjunction with an atrium that enables light to reach lower floors. However, atrium spaces may be subject to strict safety regulations that seek to minimize the spread of smoke and fire. Because of their horizontal configuration, heat loss and gain are hard to control with skylights. Skylights are most useful when placed above room areas that receive minimal amounts of natural light. Thus their most effective use is in bringing daylight to room areas farthest from windows.

In the Captain Eldridge Congregate House in Hyannis, Massachusetts, a large linear skylight, located at the central apex of a pitched roof, directs light to the middle of the building, where it is needed most (Morton 1981). Here a two-story atrium that contains a central stair and elevator allows sunlight to reach the first floor. Windows located between each unit kitchen and the atrium invite natural light. The kitchen also receives natural light from windows that face outside and, as a result, is bright and cheery.

The Horizon Club's one-story assisted living facility in Deerfield Beach, Florida, uses a collection of skylights in the center of the building above a shared lounge. The centrally located lounge is surrounded by units and contains mature plants that break up the space and add to its tropical character.

Skylights are often used in conjunction with multifloor atriums above lobby spaces, where corridors join the building entry. At the Atrium, in Boca Raton, Florida, a five-story skylight atrium links two L-shaped corridors with the entry. Three shared lounge areas serve unit clusters on a typical floor and are in full view of the atrium. The uniqueness and visibility of this multistory skylight also aid in orientation by helping residents to find their way.

Skylights can also be used to highlight areas and to order the placement of furniture. The Paddock Kensington in Beatrice, Nebraska, is an older hotel that was remodeled into assisted living housing. A skylight near the entry effectively highlights the reception desk.

In the Sunrise at Fairfax Retirement Home in Fairfax, Virginia, several large transparent skylights have been installed on the third floor above the tea room, which is used for a range of special activities. The transparent dome of each skylight allows residents to see the twig and branch patterns of surrounding mature deciduous trees that ring the site.

FIGURE 3.5. *Single loaded corridors can be widened to provide residents with an enclosed and protected balcony:* This project in Halmstad, Sweden overlooks the city center.

Daylight Applications. In large spaces such as a dining room, clerestory windows or skylights can be used to enhance the character of the space while allowing enough light for plants to grow. When coordinated with the dining room seating plan, well-placed skylights can help define spatial areas by creating pools of light within the room.

Skylights can also be used to introduce natural light into compact, enclosed, double-loaded corridors. In a one-story sheltered living facility in England, Hoglund (1985) identified a project in which skylights were located above the entry to each unit. This placement filled the corridor with natural light, allowing plants to grow in beds in front of each unit.

Tall windows can also be used to introduce light deeper into rooms and corridors. In the Elder-Homestead facility in Minnetonka, Minnesota, a large double-story panel of glass is used to create a greenhouse on one side of a corridor that connects the dining room to a cluster of units. Greenhouses as separate spaces or as wrap-around attachments to corridors can provide

enhanced natural light while introducing a very attractive visual connection
with the outdoors.

4. Use of Spatial Hierarchy

Code limitations often discourage overlapping spatial connections between
rooms and corridors in institutional occupancy buildings. This is one reason
nursing homes often consist of uniform corridors linked through firewalls to

FIGURE 3.6. *Two story entry space links the middle and upper floors:* An open
stair and open balcony rail at Rosewood Estate encourage the awareness of amenities located on the upper floor.

small, boxlike rooms. Codes that govern multistory atriums and contain provisions for more visually complex spatial connections between corridors and meeting rooms are often interpreted in ways that limit these applications. Regulations governing second-story balconies or sitting areas that overlook lively circulation spaces may require costly and unsightly wire glass enclosures.

Nursing homes often lack spatial variety, which helps to make them appear dreary, institutional, and lifeless. Occasionally, dining rooms are taller and less uniform in their spatial configuration. However, larger dining room spaces can often present a clumsy fit, instead of adding to spatial variety. They can appear institutional and have acoustical problems that impair normal conversation. Entry spaces that appear large and dramatic in height and volume can also feel impersonal and cold and resemble a commercial office building more than a residence. Spaces of varying height, proportion, and size should be used to add variety and delight without making the place appear commercial and cold. Some argue that the most effective way to communicate the feeling of a homelike environment is to keep room sizes near residential scale, between 150 and 400 square feet.

Adjusting ceiling heights is often the only way to introduce a range of spatial volumes. This is because changes in the height of floors must be accompanied by ramps that take an enormous amount of space and can result in a tripping hazard.

Stairs. An open stair not only links two floors but enhances spatial variety. Moving from one floor to another by ascending or descending a stair is a wonderful way to experience the spatial qualities of a room and its surroundings. The reliance on elevators in multistory housing and the code requirements that specify enclosed fire stairs often make additional open stairs an unnecessary and redundant expense. However, when used effectively, an open stair can provide a focal point to the entry sequence, a natural form of exercise for residents, and an opportunity to view adjacent spaces from a changing perspective.

The Sunrise Retirement Home in Fairfax, Virginia, uses a double back stair as a functional and visual focal element. With a width of 48 inches it has a residential scale and resembles the elaborate stairs characteristic of historic Victorian mansions.

Using a skylight to add natural light above a stair can increase the stair's attractiveness. A good example of this application is provided by the Captain Eldridge Congregate House described earlier.

Overlooks and Preview Spaces. The Changebridge Inn in Monteville, New Jersey, uses a large two-story atrium near the center of its commons to focus circulation and activity. Skylights in combination with clerestory windows provide enough natural light for plant materials and trees to grow.

Upper-floor overlooks adjacent to circulation pathways can allow residents to enjoy movement and activity below. In larger facilities an atrium design provides numerous opportunities for creating overlooks. It is also a powerful visual focal element, useful in helping residents find their way.

Rooms can overlap and connect through a variety of devices that allow residents the opportunity to "preview" activities before they make a commitment to enter a room. Half walls, lower ceiling soffits, windows, changes in floor and ceiling materials, overlooks, pierced plane screens, planters, furniture arrangements, and deep portal entry spaces are only a few of the ways in which spatial edges can be defined. These devices allow subtle connections between rooms as an alternative to the conventional door, and in the process they offer a rich collection of environmental experiences.

5. Site Design Considerations

A good site design should extend indoor spaces outdoors. The configuration and topography of a site often contain cues that aid in site planning and building concept development. Existing mature trees, an interesting off-site view, or a nearby park can be used to configure a building. The appearance of the building as it is first experienced from off the site is another major factor in establishing its image and is thus a major site-planning consideration.

Buildings are often perceived as either an object or a context for landscape design. An object building is located in the landscape, often in the midst of a parklike setting. Courtyard buildings create their own context or frame for landscape by bounding and defining it, usually in the form of one or more outdoor "rooms." The relationship of the building to the street and surrounding housing is most important in courtyard housing. This is common in Europe, where low-rise, high-density solutions are popular.

Site Design for Exercise and Therapy. Designing the site to encourage an active life-style requires conceptualizing outdoor spaces in the form of places where behavioral, functional, and aesthetic intentions are clearly articulated. For example, the site should support and encourage walking for exercise, possibly incorporating an extended nature walk when the size of the property is generous. A walking path at Park Place in Portland, Oregon, winds through an adjacent wooded area. At the Corinne Dolan Alzheimer's Center in Heather Hill, Ohio, a two-acre wandering park provides exercise and a sense of release for agitated dementia residents.

Site design for exercise can also be modest, involving walkways within a courtyard or sidewalks around the periphery of a facility. In an assisted living facility designed but never constructed in Fresno, California, Soderstrom Architects surrounded a courtyard on three sides with housing. The fourth side contained the dining room linked to the units by an enclosed corridor. An optional path through the courtyard allowed residents and staff a "shortcut" to the dining room and other common areas. Having two paths from a resident's room to the dining room encourages choice. Residents can stay within the protected confines of the corridor or, on a nice day, experience the courtyard outside.

Exercise rooms extended through a terrace into an adjoining courtyard encourage enjoyment of outdoor exercises when weather permits. Outdoor site features can be a source of sensory stimulation as well. At the Jewish Home for the Aged in Reseda, California, a sensory garden provides the wheelchair-bound and ambulatory resident with a garden of raised planter beds, where colorful and fragrant plant materials grow.

Mammals and small amphibians are popular in facilities for the elderly. When domestic animals are located in cages or open areas within a courtyard, visiting them provides a reason for a trip outside.

In Alzheimer facilities the idea of a "wandering" garden has become a major source of creative thinking about the therapeutic role these spaces can play. At the Motion Picture Country House and Hospital in Woodland Hills, California, an outdoor garden adjacent to the Alzheimer's unit has been designed to contain several different "ecologies." One portion of the site is planted with evergreen trees and includes a recirculating stream, evoking the feeling of a mountain area. Another portion of the garden contains an aviary, park bench, and drinking fountain centered around an open space. This area evokes the feeling of a civic park. A looped sidewalk links these various places, providing a path that allows a resident to wander through several distinct outdoor rooms.

Landscape Elements. Large trees and mature plant materials can soften building exteriors and courtyard spaces. In addition, they provide a cooling effect in the summer through transpiration and shade. At Mount San Antonio Gardens in Pomona, California, the assisted living lodge has been

FIGURE 3.7. *This Alzheimer's wandering garden is designed around several landscape themes:* An aviary, drinking fountain, park bench, babbling brook and porch swing are located along a looped walking path at the Motion Picture Country House and Hospital in Woodland Hills, CA.

constructed around a courtyard adjacent to a large California live oak tree. The oak is a prominent controlled-view feature of the courtyard and adds to its interest.

Policies that limit the size of new landscape materials to small starter plants are a major shortcoming of many new facilities. Large, colorful, and fragrant plants should always be considered. Although more expensive, they enhance the gardenlike atmosphere of the place.

Views of attractive outdoor landscaping from inside a building should be carefully considered. Such common spaces as the living room, dining room, exercise room, and lounge can be extended through exterior terraces or attractively landscaped views. The outdoor relationship with each common room should be carefully reviewed. Some facilities visually extend interior spaces through devices like greenhouse windows or window seats that serve as connectors between indoor and outdoor areas.

Landscape Concepts That Support Activities. Outdoor spaces should also support socializing and the vicarious viewing of on- and off-site activities. Comfortable, conveniently situated benches that allow older residents to sit, rest, and watch nearby activity are the basic building blocks of a successful site design strategy. Site features will not be enjoyed if shaded, interesting, and comfortable places to rest are unavailable.

Outdoor seating is often configured without much thought about the views associated with it. Opportunities to view interesting on- and off-site activities can occur in many places and therefore should be identified and pursued. The site of the Armour House in Kansas City, Missouri, was planned to capitalize on a nearby park. The outcome provides the feel of a rural setting in a very urban context. The Chambrel at Island Lake in Longwood, Florida, placed the assisted living unit so that it has views of a nearby lake. It capitalized further on the lake amenity by creating an enclosed glass porch that overlooks it.

Adequate consideration for drop-off and pick-up activities near the entry is also important, along with a covered walkway that links the drop-off area with the front door. A covered canopy or porte cochere can provide first-time visitors with cues about how to enter a building while creating a sheltered place for residents to sit and wait. Sunrise in Fairfax, Virginia, designed a second "low-key" automobile entry with an attached porte cochere.

FIGURE 3.8. *Swimming is a very therapeutic source of exercise for older residents:* In this Finnish project the swimming pool was financed jointly by the local municipality and is time shared with older people living in the surrounding community.

This design allowed the main entry to appear more residential, creating a compact and convenient automobile drop-off area for residents and their families.

Finally, outdoor activities should be encouraged that involve direct participation (e.g., gardening). For this to be successful, raised planting beds should be considered like those available at the Lincolnia House Senior Residences in Fairfax County, Virginia (see chapter 6). They can make it easier for the wheelchair-bound or those who find it difficult to bend to participate fully.

The Rudolph Steiner Fellowship Community in Spring Valley, New York, has developed a life-style orientation toward the natural environment that is present in its approach to site planning and program development. The assisted living complex is situated near the center of the community to encourage visiting and facilitate the vicarious observation of activities involving younger community members. This form of active engagement within the larger community context contrasts with site-planning solutions in many CCRCs that isolate less active frail residents by separating them from more active participants. Sometimes the design of assisted living housing fails to take full advantage of a site for what it can offer in the way of activities, aesthetics, and views.

6. Therapy and Architectural Design

The therapeutic milieu of assisted living should stress restorative health, exercise, fitness, and social interaction. Residents have a much better chance of maintaining competency and forestalling institutionalization if they follow an exercise and movement regimen. Exercise combined with physical therapy can often restore lost abilities. By the time a resident moves to a nursing home, overall competency is so diminished that true restorative health is difficult, if not impossible.

A wellness program involves maintaining careful and methodical checks on existing health while monitoring medications and special conditions. Health and wellness programs should be effective but low key, since a dominant presence can make the facility appear undesirably medical.

Encouraging Socialization. Beyond the goal of monitoring good nutrition, the purpose of group dining is to create friendships and informal exchanges between residents. Mealtimes can provide an opportunity to share problems, discuss solutions, and sharpen social skills. For assisted living to deal effectively with the therapeutic goals of wellness, fitness, and socialization, the physical environment should support these activities, making them a natural part of the life-style associated with the place.

Discovering effective new ways for residents to communicate both formally and informally often involves physical design. For example, the clustering of units in small groups or the adjacency of activities located in adjoining common rooms can encourage or discourage social exchange. The activities envisioned in each common room should be designed with an understanding of how the space can create and sustain a sense of community. When facilities are designed without broader therapeutic goals reflected in their architecture, programs and spaces appear ad hoc, without a sense of continuity or fit.

Exercise Therapy. Exercise therapy can occur in a room dedicated for this purpose or in a multipurpose room. However, an exercise room designed with equipment specifically geared to the strength, aerobic capacity, and competency requirements of assisted living residents is the best way to support an exercise theme. Multipurpose rooms with resilient floor coverings should be large enough to facilitate exercise and movement activities.

At Mount San Antonio Gardens in Pomona, California, a large multipur-

FIGURE 3.9. *Occupational therapy is a serious form of mental and physical exercise in Europe:* Residents produce rugs, place mats and jewelry which has commercial value and are sold in local boutiques.

pose space has been outfitted with exercise and physical therapy equipment. This "gym" provides a symbolic space for the restorative health program and includes enough fixed equipment and consulting personnel to provide a comprehensive program.

Another important form of exercise is walking in the facility. Hallways should be outfitted with handrails and places to rest, so that residents can exercise by walking from place to place inside the building. The garden at the Atrium in Boca Raton, Florida, has been designed to encourage older people to walk outside for exercise. Its visibility from inside attracts residents and encourages them to walk.

Swimming is an excellent form of exercise but may be too expensive for a small assisted living arrangement to finance without the benefit of additional independent or congregate units. Water therapy programs provide an effective form of exercise for residents with arthritis or other debilitating health problems.

Animal-Assisted Therapy. Therapeutic aspects of the environment can be enhanced through many innovative programs. Chapter 4 deals with management and administrative practice and outlines a number of effective therapeutic approaches designed to improve the health and fitness of residents.

Animal-assisted therapy programs, for example, can be as simple as the one instituted at the Alzheimer's Care Center, a residential facility in Gardiner, Maine. This program involves a dog shared by residents who moves freely within the facility during the day. A facility pet like this that residents can view, touch, or play with provides an interesting homelike distraction. Aviaries and fish tanks are also commonly used to bring variety and interest to nursing homes and assisted living.

Other programs might involve volunteers bringing animals in from the local community to visit with interested residents. In addition, residents may benefit from more structured or focused individual and group therapy, using animals to establish an environment conducive to open communication.

7. Residential Materials, Surfaces, and Finishes

One common mistake in the design of assisted living facilities is the specification of commercial or institutional finish and trim materials. This occurs because mid- and high-rise apartment housing complexes often use commercial-appearing windows, doors, wall finishes, and carpets. These are often specified in multistory, multifamily housing. When a facility is viewed as an "institutional" occupancy, commercial-grade surfaces, textures, and materials are often assumed.

The architect or owner may also perceive the need to specify practical low-maintenance finishes. However, nothing is more destructive to the overall character of a building than materials that give residents and visitors the impression that this is not a residential environment.

Residential Image. Because it is important to create a homelike environment, designers must carefully evaluate decisions dealing with materials, finishes, and surfaces from the standpoint of their residential image. Specifying residential materials often means selecting wood rather than rubber-based trim or using a sloped roof rather than a flat, built-up roof. It also means that traditional materials such as plaster ceilings should be considered in place of drop-in acoustical tile. Traditional residential materials like brick and stone can also symbolize residential imagery in various regions.

Material specifications often overemphasize first-time cost savings, low maintenance, cleanability and commercial sturdiness. Residentially scaled light fixtures specified in larger numbers are preferable to overscaled com-

FIGURE 3.10. *Three separate but connected building masses reduce the perceived size of this housing from the street:* Rosewood Estate was also designed as a two story building on the entry side and three stories on the lakeside to further reduce its massive appearance.

mercial fixtures. Emphasis should be on natural materials and those commonly associated with residential construction practice rather than on institutional and commercial applications.

Reduction of Noise. It is also important to reduce noise. One of the major problems with institutional environments is the overspecification of hard surfaces for ceilings, floors, and walls. Sound bounces and reverberates through corridors and common areas. Employing sound-reducing absorptive materials such as carpets, upholstered furniture, and tapestries can en hance visual character and give rooms the sonic feel of a residential space.

Residential Construction Details and Materials. Windows and doors should be consistent with those specified in residential environments. For example, small-pane wood windows are preferable to large aluminum frame commercial windows. Wood and glass doors that contain decorative elements should be considered over aluminum frame commercial doors. Entry doors are particularly important because they influence the perceived character of the setting as people approach and enter the building.

Sometimes the desire to specify a "considerate" response to a problem (e.g., a door that opens automatically) may be useful but also may be associated with an institutional or commercial application. Grocery stores, shopping centers, airports, and hospitals use sliding doors for entry and exit purposes. The lack of association with a residential environment may have a negative impact on the perception of the setting.

The conflict between making an environment appear "functional" and "normal" can cause dilemmas. A solution that solves an important functional problem may have negative psychological side effects. The optimum choice requires a thoughtful and careful analysis of the range of possible alternatives. Nowhere is this more evident than in the design of environments for the handicapped. Solutions that resolve functional problems often do so by creating a stigma. The universal design movement seeks to employ solutions that enhance safety and manipulation for all populations while destigmatizing these modifications (AARP 1993).

Environmental Meaning. Different rooms within residential environments are imbued with meaning through the finishes, furnishings, and surface materials used in these spaces. Bathrooms, bedrooms, and living rooms use specific floor, ceiling, and wall treatments to define each space. Each common room should have a specific character and range of purposes

FIGURE 3.11. *Translucent sconce fixtures are often used for corridor lighting:* The light from single source fixtures can be uneven and may create glare but they reinforce the residential character of the setting.

that inspire definition and meaning. The more we understand about how a space is to be used, the more likely it is that the interior fixtures, furnishings, finishes, and materials will reinforce that concept. Monotony can result from grouping sofas, low tables, and chairs in available left-over space. Using couches and chairs indiscriminately results in an overall appearance that is devoid of meaning. This "overlounging" creates a blandness that subtracts from the facility's character.

Late-nineteenth-century country homes often used several different rooms for entertaining and socializing. Each was created with a specific purpose in mind. The breakfast room, formal dining room, library, billiards parlor, sewing room, and conservatory were designed around specific activities and commonly held beliefs. Materials, furnishings, and textures associated with activities in these rooms formed a distinct image or character for each room.

Applications. Developing residential references from the features and qualities of older housing stock can avoid an institutional look while reflecting the history of housing in that region. The Mary Conrad Center in Anchorage, Alaska, has attempted this by specifying ornately carved trim pieces in the design of half-walls and balustrades that communicate a residential image and reflect the history of this rugged territory.

The Captain Eldridge Congregate House in Hyannis, Massachusetts, uses hardwood flooring; wooden chairs and tables; a small, residentially scaled breakfast room; and classic cape cod details on balcony railings to reinforce its residential character. The intimately scaled formal parlor and living room from the original 2,000-square-foot nineteenth-century home were preserved, lending an authentic scale and character to the shared spaces. A number of lessons clearly visible in this facility involve special sensitivity toward selecting materials and design details that allow an 8,000-square-foot addition to complement the original architecture.

8. Exterior Design Considerations

Designing the exterior envelope of a building involves arriving at a massing configuration sensitive to site and context, selecting architectural details and elements that reinforce residential references, choosing a palette of compatible colors, specifying appropriate residential materials, and developing an idea about how landscape elements will be expressed. This is one of the most important challenges an architect faces in designing assisted living housing.

Residential Scale. A refined massing configuration should be chosen that is sensitive to residential scale and does not overwhelm residents. For most situations this will involve a structure of less than three stories. Scale, however, is also relative to context. In a neighborhood of single-family, one-story houses, a three-story dwelling may appear too big. Conversely, a three-story building in the center of a city surrounded by high-rise housing may seem quite intimate.

The term **architectural scale** also refers to the cognitive process of perceiving the relative size of a building and its component parts. In general, residential environments are perceived with reference to "standard" elements that permit an understanding of how large things are in comparison to one another. Residential doors, for example, are 6 feet, 8 inches high. Ceiling heights are frequently established at 8 feet. These accepted standards establish conceptual measures for comprehending the size of a building. Certain aspects of exterior design also provide universal cues and suggestions about residential form. Sloping roofs and fireplace chimneys are elements children often abstract to represent their concept of a house. Within interior spaces, furniture also plays a role in establishing an understanding of room size.

Front Porches, Dormers, and Balconies. The front porch is an architectural element that reduces the perceived massiveness of a building while providing a convenient, engaging place to watch on- and off-site activities. An excellent example of a well-positioned porch is provided by the three-season enclosed porch at the Elder-Homestead project in Minnetonka, Minnesota, which overlooks a city park. Here a parlor space has been linked to

FIGURE 3.12. *Three-season enclosed porch overlooks an adjacent park:* This porch at Elder-Homestead can be ventilated in the summer.

the porch in an effort to increase its viability and convenience. Just as a one-story porch can reduce the perceived scale of a building from the street, an upper-floor dormer can have a similar effect. Sunrise Retirement Home in Fairfax, Virginia, and Fox Hills Village in Westwood, Massachusetts, both utilize an upper floor framed as a dormer with a sloping mansard roof, to foreshorten the height of the building. This treatment bestows a character consistent with the image of the surrounding historic housing stock.

Designing an exterior that is articulated rather than flat can increase its visual interest. Grouping units in clusters can establish a massing configuration that adds to a building's spatial variety. Balconies can also increase the complexity and variety of a building's exterior. Balconies added to Changebridge Inn in Monteville, New Jersey, allow it to resemble the local surrounding housing stock in form and character.

Residential Stylistic Expression. Selecting a residential housing expression that is present in the historic building stock of a region can offer a useful point of departure for design. In New England this may be the country house, whereas in the South references may come from the "colonial" plantation house. In the West the ranch house, California bungalow, or Spanish revival courtyard house offers a rich assortment of indoor and outdoor spaces. In the Midwest large turn-of-the-century houses with front porches and partially exposed stone basements are dominant images in many older neighborhoods. These vernacular forms of residential architecture have rich interpretive possibilities and offer a comfortable and familiar stylistic palette.

Reflecting on the nature of vernacular precedents can also reveal aspects of these housing types that connote charm and comfort. Buildings of vapid character, ambiguous scale, and ambivalent aesthetic interest bring with them negative associations that remind older people of the institutions they seek to avoid. Because most older people want to live in a homelike environment, ways of capturing those qualities that are consistent with the image of home in the building form and the exterior design treatment must be considered.

Sunrise Retirement Home in Fairfax, Virginia, chose a mansion house precedent and developed an L-shaped building configuration that utilizes a front porch and dormer roof as intervening scale elements. The forty-seven-unit development was purposely limited in size to achieve a comfortable residential scale.

Hotels, especially those located near the central business districts of smaller cities and towns, have been popular as targets for adaptive reuse. (The financing chapter details some of the economic incentives that have

FIGURE 3.13. *Skylights planned in conjunction with planters create opportunities for garden landscaping:* This interior corridor is enlivened by landscape
materials and natural light.

encouraged this movement.) These buildings are often subjects of historic
preservation grants and provide residents an authentic and attractive environment. Because many of these facilities are as old as the resident population they serve, they offer a familiar, attractive character that may have special meaning.

9. Visitation for the Family

One of the tragic consequences of institutionalization is the detachment that
often occurs between family members and the older institutionalized individual. Nursing homes, the majority of which offer shared, two-bed rooms,
have relatively few common areas where family members can feel at home
when they visit. Visiting becomes an experience more like going to a hospital than to "grandma's place." In fact, new hospitals are often better designed for visitor use, with a cafeteria, flower shop, reading room, convenience store, and lounge space available (Malkin 1992). In pediatric and
maternity wards, visiting behaviors are reinforced by policies that encourage family members to stay overnight.

Nursing homes rarely contain spaces where family members feel wel-

FIGURE 3.14. *Housing for frail community residents is attached to the nursing home:* Six units of housing for independent but frail older people open to an entry courtyard adjacent to this Dnaish nursing home.

come. Even in the best facilities a "visitation space" near the front entry is often the only place available for family interaction. In many facilities family visits occur in a small, unimaginatively furnished room that resembles a sterile, impersonal lounge rather than an inviting living room.

The environment can make family members feel welcome in a number of ways. For example, larger, private units facilitate the option of inviting family members for overnight stays.

Unit Designs That Support Families. Rosewood Estate in Roseville, Minnesota, offers large one-bedroom units that can accommodate overnight stays. In other facilities separate rooms are set aside for overnight guests. In Broadmore Court, a forty-five-unit facility in Colorado Springs, Colorado, a 650-square-foot guest home has been located above the manager's office, linked to the resident building by a bridge. This unit accommodates family members and is evidence of management's interest in involving the resident's family.

One major environmental influence on family involvement is the range, amount, and type of common space available for family interaction. Borden Court, in Rochester Hills, Michigan, offers several interesting places where family members and residents can take a meal, have a conversation, or become involved in a shared activity. All these places provide opportunities for social exchange.

Hospitality Areas. Locating informal lounges for residents and their families in an active area of the building, offering a hospitality bar with coffee and soft drinks, orienting the room to an interesting view, and providing a range of places to sit (tables, chairs, sofas) can make a place attractive and fun. In settings like this, family members feel comfortable and look forward to visiting, thus becoming a more active participant in their parent's or grandparent's life.

The idea of involving family members in more supportive ways is behind the Planetree Unit, an experimental hospital ward at the Pacific Presbyterian Medical Center, in San Francisco, California. Here a social lounge and galley kitchen were created for family members and visitors, through the remodeling of a conventional nurses station. A side benefit of reducing space for nursing and charting activities was the creation of a more open and friendly nurses station plan. Patients who would like a home-prepared meal

FIGURE 3.15. *The Planetree unit humanizes acute care hospital wards:* This installation at Presbyterian Medical Center in San Francisco, CA, has a small kitchen where families of patients can prepare snacks and special home cooked meals.

can have it catered by family members. Although not encouraged, the lounge space can also accommodate overnight stays.

Family-Care Provision. Case management and service assessment models of care provision have allowed family members to play a more substantive role in helping with various activities. Rackleff House in Canby, Oregon, uses a case management system that invites family members to help care for residents. Both Rackleff House and Daystar in Seattle, Washington, have resident laundry rooms where family activities and interactions are encouraged around the traditional task of doing laundry.

Borden Court in Rochester Hills, Michigan, has also taken the symbolic step of providing family members with keys to unit clusters within the facility. This required extensive negotiations with regulatory officials. The facility was able to argue that the benefits of making family members feel welcome outweighed minimal security risks.

A relatively common approach to family involvement is through group events that allow the relatives and friends of residents to meet one another. These events also allow the family to meet and socialize with staff and administration in an informal, friendly setting. Palmcrest Home in Long Beach, California, organizes family events around various themes. An informal summer barbecue uses outdoor and indoor spaces to accommodate a large number of people that attend this event.

10. Codes and Regulations

Assisted living facilities are generally regulated by state governments under board-and-care laws that vary by state (AAHA 1992). Regulations are often written to fit a range of facility sizes, from small foster care arrangements to large stand-alone facilities. Typically, state governments classify assisted living as a "board and care" rather than a health care facility. Thus they can avoid the narrow, physical design and staffing requirements to which nursing homes must conform.

Regulations Often Restrict Design Expression. To define the differences between assisted living and nursing care, states have relied primarily on indicators of resident competency. In some states incontinence indicates nursing home candidacy, even though most experts agree this is not a condition that requires around-the-clock health care supervision. In other states patients confined to a wheelchair may also be prematurely institutionalized. Many state regulations consider anyone who needs an assistive device (cane, walker, four-prong cane) or anyone who experiences confusion in getting around the facility to be nonambulatory. Facilities designed for the "nonambulatory" must meet additional standards for exiting and safety.

From a building code perspective the design and construction of multistory facilities often require that standards for I (institutional) occupancies be achieved in the design of facilities. These standards are similar to those used to construct nursing homes. Facilities constructed under I occupancies may cost as much as $10 a square foot more to build and may require materials that appear less residential.

Requirements may be based on the false assumption that residents are bedfast, typically requiring an 8-foot-wide corridor and a 44-inch door, so that they can be moved while prone in a single bed. Code considerations like these were developed years ago in response to fire safety protocols in buildings without sprinklers. Patients were typically evacuated through corridors during a fire. To accommodate this, doors needed to be wide enough to move a bed through and corridors had to be wide enough for two beds to pass. New fire-fighting methods isolate residents in their rooms rather than moving them through smoke-filled corridors.

Assisted living housing typically does not have bedfast residents and should not be expected to meet this standard. Confusion about the competency level of patients and a conservative attitude that errs on the side of caution have led to these regulatory interpretations.

Local Officials Are Less Sophisticated. An additional complication involves the review, classification, and assessment of buildings by local fire departments. If local officials view assisted living as an institution, they may not be willing to grant any exception that might hamper fire fighters or increase the vulnerability of the building to fire and smoke damage. Local fire officials are often unaware of the range of code exceptions routinely granted for sprinklered buildings of this occupancy type. However, stringent code interpretations can eliminate such homelike features as fireplaces, open stairs, atriums, and open connections between common spaces and corridors.

Sponsors consider many code interpretations overly harsh. It is difficult to reason with code officials over building requirements when the argument involves comparing the intangible issues of appearance and character with an objective concern for safety. However, the institutional appearance resulting from narrow interpretations impacts visitors, family members, and staff, and in many cases it affects the way residents view themselves. The result is the warehousing of older residents in ugly institutional boxes that

FIGURE 3.16. *Overlapping spaces add to spatial complexity and hierarchy:* Plant materials and horizontal bars are used in this courtyard atrium in Finland. Conservative fire code restrictions limit atrium applications in the United States.

are nonetheless quite safe. European facilities have managed to avoid many of these conflicts and often produce very residential-appearing designs that would not be sanctioned under U.S. codes.

Risk assessment needs to balance cost and character against the probability of injury. The safety record for facilities is complicated by incidents in antiquated nursing homes and board-and-care housing grandfathered under codes that do not meet even the most minimal standards of care.

In a number of states, sponsors have challenged the regulations by organizing assisted living facilities as conventional apartments with services delivered by a separate "arm's-length" agreement with a home health agency. This approach allows the facility to skirt overly harsh code requirements. The buildings that result have few special safety considerations other than what would normally be required for apartment construction.

Regulatory Reform and Exceptions. New regulations relaxing some of the harsher code constraints for assisted living housing are currently being pursued in a number of states. This will help to clarify misconceptions by local officials who have difficulty interpreting whether or not a building should be constructed under a residential (R) or institutional (I) occupancy type. States like Oregon and Washington have worked closely with community care regulators to develop interpretations leading to cost-effective building standards. Differences in code interpretation by state and the conflicting requirements of local fire and building codes have led the Environmental Design Clearinghouses to identify innovative code exceptions and offer a rational third-party assessment of code problems for sponsors who have received overly harsh interpretations.

Typically, assisted living facilities are granted narrower corridor widths (6 feet instead of 8 feet) and narrower entry doors (36 inches instead of 44 inches) than generally required in institutional settings. Some states have also developed fire sprinkler codes that allow multistory atriums and open stairs. Others have permitted ramps to second-floor levels to suffice as exits. Still others allow fireplaces in rooms, with magnetic closures that can be activated if a fire or smoke problem arises.

The fuzzy relationship between assisted living and nursing homes and the tradition of placing personal care units within the "health center" of multilevel continuing-care facilities has hampered the definition of assisted living as a residential housing type. The next five years will likely produce federal guidelines and standards and bring about greater uniformity. It is hoped that new requirements will consider the need to balance attitudes about health and safety rationally with the need to create a more residential-appearing and less expensive form of supportive housing for the older frail person.

11. Common, Recreational, and Social Spaces

Various social, recreational, educational, and therapeutic activities occur within shared common spaces. This range of activities should lead to differences in common spaces that reflect variety in their character, appearance, size, and furnishings.

FIGURE 3.17. *Greenhouse window provide daylight, orientation cues and increased spatial variety:* Located adjacent to an upper floor residential corridor at the Villa Marin in San Rafael, CA, the enclosure provides a place for residents to sit, rest and socialize.

One frequent mistake in designing common rooms is to fail to give each space a clear purpose. This happens when spaces are labeled and furnished without a sense of how they are likely to serve their purposes. Furnishings often inappropriately "decorate" a space rather than define the scale, purpose, orientation, and proportion of a room.

Strive for Uniqueness of Purpose. Facilities in search of a consistent image may create too many spaces that look and feel alike. This can result in areas that are either too formal and elegant or too casual and uniform. Normal residential environments typically contain rooms of varying formality, each with distinct behavioral expectations. The parlor and the kitchen vary in their appearance and in the type of social activity they support. Imagining the variety and character of activities to be carried out in the space can help specify the colors, materials, textures, furnishings, capacity, character, appearance, acoustical liveliness, light levels, and fixtures needed.

Another planning and design shortcoming is a lack of awareness about how spaces are used at different times of the day and during different seasons of the year. In contrast to the strategy of assigning a specific function or purpose to each room is an approach that anticipates how spaces might be combined, separated, or transformed for special events and ongoing programs. Both of these design strategies require "rehearsing" the patterns of use and the purposes of various settings. This exercise avoids the monotonous outcome in facilities where each space appears to support the same limited range of passive pursuits. Design strategies should strive for a better understanding of purpose in defining the use and appearance of various spaces.

Furnishing Items and Scale. The use of accessories and unique furnishings to imbue different rooms with interest and variety is underexplored. Limiting the choice of furnishings to what is available in the catalogs of commercial furniture manufacturers creates monotony. Although the risk in such an approach is minimal, so is the gain.

Selecting an appropriate scale for various common rooms can be difficult. Although the single-family house is the reference model, the assisted living dining room must accommodate a larger number of residents than would typically be present in a single-family house. Achieving a homelike feeling in a larger room is difficult.

Sunrise Retirement Home on Mercer Island, Washington, has created several residentially scaled rooms where furnishings are used to establish individual character. The size of its rooms is similar to what one would expect in a large house. The organization of units in clusters also encourages a decentralized pattern of resident activities. The size of the dining room here has been minimized by planning two seatings and by careful attention to the room's proportions.

Elder-Homestead in Minnetonka, Minnesota, has created a residentially scaled parlor near its front entry. A fireplace, bay window, and long furnishing wall in conjunction with a portal entry to the room create three logical places for furniture groupings. Thus a residential scale is maintained while the room serves to support three relatively autonomous conversation areas.

FIGURE 3.18. *Handicapped access requirements require large bathrooms:* Ambulatory residents can use this space for storage by installing demountable cabinets.

All these room examples have been designed, proportioned, and furnished to be in scale with residential references.

Alcoves, Fireplaces, and Furnishings. Another approach to creating smaller intimate rooms is to attach alcove spaces to a larger room, thereby increasing the capacity of a room while defining more intimate areas for social exchange or special-use activities. At Brighton Gardens in Sun City, Arizona, a small alcove adjacent to the main living room lounge is used as an intimate reading room.

Fireplaces are often used as a focus for clarifying a room's purpose. The Elder-Homestead project, Borden Court, and Rosewood Estate have all created rooms that use the fireplace as an organizing element.

At Borden Court corridors have been given street names to simplify orientation and build upon the metaphor of the street as a lively public environment. To reinforce its street imagery common spaces have been linked to corridors through false-storefront façades. Where space permits, movable chairs and tables have been placed in corridors to imbue them with more life. This approach allows the compact, double-loaded corridor to become a support system for a range of activities as well as a link between common rooms.

Selecting room locations with good visual accessibility to on- and off-site views is particularly important. At Sunrise in Fairfax, Virginia, the dining room location was selected because of the off-site views it afforded. The dining room is one space where residents can be expected to sit for an extended period, two to three times each day. Variety in the seating arrangement and type of view available adds to the positive experience of taking a meal.

A common practice in European facilities that do not contain a full kitchen in each unit is to provide a shared group kitchen that can be used for informal social events or intimate family get-togethers. At Brighton Gardens in Sun City, Arizona, a shared kitchen is located adjacent to a small dining room that can be reserved by residents for special events or used as an informal gathering place.

Antique furniture selected to reflect the regional history of a surrounding area can stimulate positive past recollections while adding variety and interest. At the Argyle in Denver, Colorado, two hundred pieces of antique furniture have been used in rooms and corridors to add a touch of historic character and interest. At Sunrise Retirement Home in Frederick, Maryland, artwork has been selected especially for its affective value. Portraits, landscapes, animals, and scenes of people allow the artwork to add a layer of emotional content to corridors and public spaces.

12. Corridors and Connecting Spaces

The difficulties in ambulation experienced by a majority of assisted living residents have led to an emphasis on short, efficient, and compact corridor configurations. Facilities often employ dense double-loaded corridors without windows to link residential units with common spaces. The resulting corridor pattern can be confusing and disorienting. Single-loaded corridors

FIGURE 3.19. *This column design creates an effective portal to residential units beyond:* Located on the upper floor of the Elder-Homestead project, it reduces the perceived length of the corridor.

with windows on one side are less efficient and typically more expensive. Conceptualized as an active connecting "street," the corridor can be a stimulating space. More often than not, however, it is a bleak, long extrusion broken only by unit entry doors.

A range of improvements and adjustments to the corridor can give it more life and greater interest. Some of the most effective improvements are simple. For example, corridors should be broken and offset periodically, as well as limited in length. The Sunrise retirement housing communities in Arlington and Fairfax are both designed with compact double-loaded corridors that are never longer than 20 feet (Bowe 1990). When a corridor breaks in direction, daylight should be introduced with a view to aid resident orientation. Clustering unit entry doors, dropping the ceiling height of the corridor in front of entry doors, and placing alcoves around unit entries can make a corridor seem shorter.

Personalization at the Entry. The unit entry can be made more personal by decorating it to resemble the front door of a single-family home. An alcove, package shelf, doorbell, light, exterior panel door design, and address are homelike features that can be added.

At the Corrine Dolan Alzheimer's Center in Heather Hill, Ohio, each unit entry is flanked by a small enclosed showcase where photos or personal objects are displayed for orientation and recognition purposes. These items help confused residents to identify the entry door to their room more easily.

Hoglund (1985) recorded an excellent example of an enclosed, double-loaded corridor where self-expression at the unit edge was employed in a sheltered housing project in England. Brick facing, a storage cabinet for milk, a sisal mat in front of the door, a bench/plant shelf, a dropped wood ceiling, and a change in the floor material were used to add variety and individuality to each unit entry. These features provided many opportunities for residents to personalize their unit entry.

Dutch Doors and Windows. Dutch doors have been used in some facilities to link units with corridors. At the Lutheran Home in Arlington Heights, Illinois, Dutch doors are employed in a nursing unit to allow staff to communicate with residents without keeping residents' doors continually propped open. The Dutch door design provides an added sense of privacy. At the Captain Eldridge Congregate House, Elder-Homestead, and Woodside Place, Dutch doors are used to connect private units to adjacent "semipublic" spaces. Their use creates a better social linkage between units and adjacent spaces. Sadly, code considerations regarding smoke containment in nursing facilities have limited the use of this very effective device.

Windows between the unit and the corridor are also very effective in creating a social connection to the corridor and to other neighbors. Single-loaded exterior corridors are relatively common in independent housing for the elderly. When they are employed, these corridors function as semipublic spaces where plants and movable furniture are displayed. In enclosed corridors fire codes normally reduce the amount and type of glass permissible between the unit and the corridor. The Captain Eldridge Congregate House was able to classify its facility in a way that eliminated the need for a wall with a one-hour fire rating between units and the central atrium. In doing so, the zone between the unit and the shared semipublic space was allowed to develop as an informal "front porch," open yet protected. At Eaton Terrace in Lakewood, Colorado, sidelights located adjacent to the corridor were placed in an effort to link galley kitchens in each unit with the enclosed double-loaded corridor.

Natural Light and Unit Clusters. Bringing natural light to a corridor is often hard to achieve except in single-story housing, where skylights can often be added at minimal expense. The Palmcrest Home in Long Beach,

California, has used skylights in combination with track lighting to emphasize artwork located throughout corridors.

A good example of a creative corridor plan is provided by the Terraces of Los Gatos in Los Gatos, California (Regnier, Hoglund, and Klaasen 1993). In this plan SMP architects purposefully clustered four doors and offset the entrance to each unit with a modest alcove. Lighting was increased, the ceiling dropped, and the color of floor coverings changed to define the set of four entry doors as a node of activity. This type of treatment brings attention to portions of the corridor and helps to make a long corridor appear shorter, and it encourages friendships between neighbors.

13. Linking to the Community

Residents who move to assisted living often fear their move will begin a gradual disengagement from the broader community. Connections with the surrounding community that increase resident engagement can diminish this fear.

Several strategies come to mind to accomplish this. Most involve non-physical "program" approaches that attract outside groups to the facility. However, approaches that involve mixing land uses on the same site continue to be some of the most intriguing solutions. Day-care centers for children, adult day-care programs, senior centers, and mixed-use retail complexes have been popular co-location strategies. These varied land uses generate unusual on-site activity patterns connecting the facility with other groups of people.

Another strategy involves providing on-site services to the surrounding community. This can include an informal gesture such as offering a meeting space for a local community group or a neighborhood polling place for elections. More formal approaches may involve developing an on-site restaurant open to the public as well as to residents. This idea can be controversial if traffic studies require parking spaces to accommodate outsiders. A particularly clever approach to this idea is being experimented with at the Sunrise retirement community at Falls Church, Virginia. The ice cream parlor on the first floor has a separate door to the outside and has been designed so that community residents can be invited into the space when services at an adjacent church are over on Sunday afternoons.

A third category involves providing services off-site to older people living within the surrounding community. Diversified facilities serving the surrounding neighborhood have developed home-care agencies, nurses registries, and recruitment agencies for home-care personnel. A popular approach is to share the kitchen as a preparation site for community meals-on-wheels programs.

Land Use Strategies. The Sunrise Retirement Home in Fairfax, Virginia, has created a preschool and day school for children on the same site as its forty-seven-unit facility. The school program has been used in intergenerational activities at Sunrise. It is also an incentive to attract employees with preschool-age children.

Lincolnia House in Fairfax, Virginia (see chapter 6), exemplifies a housing project co-located with a senior center and adult day-care facility. Created by the Fairfax County Housing Authority, it provides subsidized housing to an older, frail, low-income population. A courtyard separates the newly constructed housing from an adaptively reused elementary school that contains senior center activities. Co-locating these facilities allows program activities and facilities to be shared with the community. This concept is similar to that on which many of the European service centers are based that service the health and social service needs of the surrounding neighborhood population, as well as residents living in adjacent sheltered housing (Regnier 1993; Regnier 1994).

FIGURE 3.20. *Project constructed above a parking garage:* The Heritage House, in downtown Seattle, WA is located in an air rights zone above parking for the historic Pike Place Market.

Urban locations with excellent access to services are often difficult to locate. In Seattle an air-rights site above the popular and colorful Pike Place Market was used for Heritage House, a subsidized assisted living project. The low demand for parking and the idea of integrating housing into this context was intriguing to the housing authority that developed the project jointly with a nonprofit sponsor.

Palmcrest, in Long Beach, California, also contains an art gallery. During the last ten years, numerous artists have displayed their work here to residents, families, and visitors. An acquisition policy allows artists free gallery exhibition space in exchange for a contribution of artwork to the facility. Acquisitions are located throughout the facility, enhancing its character. This theme has also been pursued in the form of an art therapy program for residents.

Locating various mixed land uses near assisted living housing links the facility to the broader community, makes it more approachable, and decreases its isolation.

Conclusions

The following outline a few of the major issues where the design of the environment plays a major role: residential and institutional models; range of unit types; clustering units; importance of the site; and people, place, and activity.

1. Residential and Institutional Models

The overall physical appearance, configuration, and scale of assisted living housing has been influential in defining it as a residential long-term-care alternative. Institutional and residential models currently coexist, often serving the same resident population. This report has sought to identify the buildings that appear most residential and that support the frailest population. The word *residential* has been used not only to describe the homelike qualities of the physical environment but also to identify a management style that focuses on keeping residents as independent as possible in a context that delivers the maximum amount of privacy and choice.

2. Range of Unit Types

The size and the types of space included within a typical unit are surprisingly varied. Some units do not include kitchen appliances, whereas in others a kitchen with basic food preparation equipment is required to support a wide range of domestic activities. Current thinking is to create larger units with more amenities. Units with 300 to 500 square feet are becoming more common and may replace those with 200 to 300 square feet in the future.

3. Clustering Units

The concept and utility of using unit clusters as a basic building block for social organization is well understood and appreciated. Cluster plans often lead to more social exchange, greater informal helping behavior, a higher degree of interdependence, and therefore more friendships. Another side benefit of clustering units is the additional complexity in the building configuration that can give it more character and reinforce feelings of residential scale. Clustering units in ways that support these basic goals make the housing friendlier.

4. Importance of the Site

A surprising number of projects have disappointing site plans with few relationships to outdoor spaces that support passive or active uses. The outdoor environment, especially in Sun Belt states, can be a major source of stimulation for the mind, body, and spirit. Sense-stimulating plant materials, outdoor exercise therapy, retreat spaces, an area to watch others, ties to the surrounding neighborhood, and the beauty and connection to natural ecology are all offered by designs that embrace the possibilities of site integration.

5. People, Place, and Activity

The success of an assisted living environment depends on the physical setting (place), the resident population (people), and the activities that are manifested in interactions between people and places. All three are necessary conditions for a successful environment. The physical environment plays an important role in setting the stage for activity and instrumentally supporting, enhancing, and stimulating a range of positive behaviors.

Challenges for the Future

Although many possibilities exist for future change in adjusting assisted living models, the following seem the most promising: residential image, therapeutic environments, code constraints, and the involvement of families.

1. Residential Image

One of the major architectural challenges of designing an assisted living residence is to recall, support, and simulate the feelings associated with a residential environment. The consistent major complaint about the architecture of these settings is that they rely on institutional models. The appearance, furnishings, room sizes, relationships between major common spaces, and materials specified for interior finishes greatly affect a building's residential character. The single largest challenge architects face in designing these facilities is creating an attractive residential setting that is large enough to meet economy-of-scale requirements for efficient, functional service production.

2. Therapeutic Environments

One basic difference between an assisted living facility and a skilled nursing facility is the promise it holds as an effective therapeutic environment. Although nursing homes have therapy equipment, we rarely think of them as having a strong focus in this domain. In assisted living, therapy in the form of mental stimulation, physical activity, social interaction, and spiritual encouragement is an assumed part of the daily regimen. Environments must be sensitive to this goal and thus provide opportunities for this type of stimulation. Environments that stop at the point of providing only support and do not challenge an individual's latent abilities are only prosthetic and are not delivering truly therapeutic opportunities to residents.

3. Code Constraints

The confusion brought about by conflicting code requirements has major impacts on the homelike appearance of the setting and the cost of construction. No one questions the need to construct a safe environment for older frail persons. The debate centers on (1) how safe the facilities must be and at what point overlapping safety systems become redundant and therefore waste resources and (2) how these systems affect the appearance of the facility and the life-style possible there. Facilities that have fire sprinklers and have an efficient protocol for fire system maintenance and upkeep virtually eliminate the potential problems associated with a facility fire. Narrowly interpreted code considerations greatly affect opportunities for introducing natural light through skylights and atriums and for creating more socially stimulating connections between the corridor and each unit. Other countries operating under similar ethical concerns and providing environments for equally frail individuals have overcome this problem with greater cooperation and a broader view toward creating environments that offer residents safe and humane design alternatives.

4. Involvement of Families

Among the most important priorities in designing housing for frail people is the need to involve families in their care. Often older people are institutionalized because a family-centered system of care breaks down or the older person's needs outpace the ability of family members to meet them. Assisted living can be treated as an extension of the family care system that involves additional provision for formal care. However, many regulations under which facilities operate preclude negotiations and arrangements with family members for sharing the care burden. One of the most attractive attributes of home health care is the ability it provides to establish a care plan that helps the family to cope with the problems of an older family member.

We must explore housing arrangements and licensing regulations that allow this level of flexibility if we expect family members to continue to be active participants in the older person's life. Passing the responsibility of care and management is now like passing a baton at a relay race. It is the total shifting of responsibility from the family to the institution that seems entirely wrong. No one expects a children's day-care center or elementary school to take total responsibility for nurturing the dependent young. Similarly, the family should be involved in the care of an older member. Therefore we need to embrace models of providing care for the elderly that allow for this participation. The environment can be an important component of this program by providing space where family members can feel a sense of belonging.

The next three to five years will be very important in defining, establishing, and testing new models of assisted living that deliver more humane, therapeutic, family-centered and choice-laden combinations of housing and services.

4. Managing a Therapeutic Environment

It is sometimes difficult to convince people that the frail elderly can live in an unrestricted environment. This is partly due to the assumption that their only alternative when their need for personal care increases is a nursing home. This publication aims to destroy that assumption by demonstrating how assisted living housing can return freedom of choice, dignity, independence, privacy, and individuality to older frail people.

The fundamentals of human nature should not be ignored when an assisted living facility is being designed. All people need to feel control over their lives and environment. As they age, many find their roles as workers and contributing family members diminish as their physical capabilities and income decline. The best policy is to keep the elderly as an integral part of the community and help them remain as independent as possible. The goal of the World Health Organization describes this succinctly:

> The keystone of policies on aging is the commitment of all sectors of government, of non-governmental organizations, of caring professions and of individual programs aimed at the promotion of health and the maintenance of functioning during aging. . . . services should not generate dependency, and paternalistic practices which erode independence should be discarded. An explicit objective of health policies should help aging persons maintain the maximum degree of independent life in the face of increasing difficulty in performing daily activities [United Nations 1982].

Management Responsibilities

Management is the process of working with and through other people to accomplish the objectives of an organization. The basic functions of a manager include planning, organizing, coordinating, orchestrating, and evaluating day-to-day life.

Management sets the tone for a facility, providing operational stability, dictating the standard of care for residents, and emphasizing the empowerment of each resident. The manager of an assisted living environment must be a caring, patient, and compassionate person, as well as a skillful business manager. The most successful operations are those in which management personnel consider themselves team leaders rather than authoritarian order givers. A nonhierarchical team approach encourages innovation, experimentation, versatility, flexibility, and responsible behavior from staff members. A structured, hierarchical, bureaucratic management system often results in narrow, rules-oriented, uncreative staff behavior. The most important element of a management philosophy is a commitment to the values associated with assisted living, such as individuality, dignity, and independence.

Terry Klaassen of Sunrise Retirement Homes has identified the following four employee traits as important for success as a Sunrise staff member:

1. Sensitivity.
2. Nurturance.
3. Support.
4. Organizational ability.

Desirable Traits for Assisted Living

Other desirable traits for assisted living staff include the following:

- A responsible character.
- Flexibility.
- Imagination.
- Good interpersonal and communication skills.
- Good listening and problem-solving skills.
- An ability to manage people individually and in groups.
- A teamwork orientation rather than a focus on personal recognition.

Skills are also important but often can be taught.

Desirable Knowledge and Experience

Knowledge and experience in the following areas are useful and desirable:

- Knowledge and belief in the mission and philosophy of the organization.
- Understanding the assisted living industry and dedication toward ensuring its growth and success.
- Understanding how state and federal regulations apply to assisted living.
- Awareness of community resources.
- Experience (or training) to handle emergency situations.
- Counseling skills for individuals and groups.
- Ability to assess the mental and emotional status of residents.
- Ability to assess the functional ability of residents.
- Awareness of life cycle issues of older people and their families.
- Understanding group dynamics.

Curiously missing from this long list are the standard responsibilities one might expect to encounter in a nursing home job description. Sunrise personnel managers go so far as to discourage the employment of aides, order-

FIGURE 4.1. *Case assessment procedures establish a unique service prescription for each resident:* This process allows individual competencies to be identified and reinforced.

lies, and nurses who have been trained in conventional nursing homes. According to Paul Klaassen, it takes enormous effort to unlearn past habits and behaviors. The major difficulty lies in the attitudes employees have about how to care for residents. Nursing home personnel are not taught to value privacy, devote individual attention to residents, reward initiative, encourage therapy, or promote engagement. Furthermore, the hierarchical system of task distribution and management encourages employees to focus more on the job task than on the people who are to be served. This approach may be successful for auto mechanics dealing with car repairs, but taking care of older people involves nurturing their minds and spirits as well as attending to their immediate personal needs.

Regulatory Considerations

Management practices in assisted living are influenced and sometimes directed by regulatory considerations. The level of support services and supervision provided to residents, ensuring safety and care standards, is a general public welfare concern. When government reimbursements for services rendered are involved, it becomes a public policy concern.

Although not directly regulated by the federal government, assisted living is generally licensed by each state. Licensing procedures and standards vary, since the agencies that may be involved in enforcement include the local Building Department, the state Fire Marshal's Office, the state Unit on Aging, the Department of Public and Mental Health, and the Department of Public Welfare/Social Service. Licensing boards in some states have recognized assisted living as a separate level of service. Associated regulations prescribe more requirements than board-and-care facilities but not as much as a skilled nursing facility.

Misinterpretations among service providers also cloud regulatory issues. An organization embracing a medical model of care could dictate guidelines that restrict creativity and innovation. Individuals and administrators may follow these policies without challenging their validity.

Management goes beyond the administration of everyday services to include ensuring resident satisfaction. Until recently, nursing facilities were primarily need driven, like hospitals. As a result, regulations have generally not been sensitive to the desires and interests of clients. Service providers in the assisted living industry are increasingly embracing a more customer-oriented philosophy that challenges the restrictive thinking of the past. These service providers are challenging outmoded regulations and seeking to provide an environment that meets the desires and the needs of its residents.

FIGURE 4.2. *Windows with low sill heights allow residents in bed or seated to see outside:* Brighton Gardens in Virginia Beach, VA has made planting areas visible from each unit.

As future residents are given alternatives, many are likely to opt for the setting that advocates more independence. A major concern for assisted living industry administrators therefore is that the industry not be overregulated. Rules and policies have negatively affected skilled nursing facilities by restricting innovation and emphasizing safety at the expense of quality of life. Since regulations are influenced by public opinion and the abuses of a free market, sponsors must strive to provide a setting consumers appreciate because it meets their needs better.

Categories of Management Focus

The twelve environment-behavior principles described in chapter 1 provide a base for combining management philosophy with the design of the building. The following categories of management practices were defined as a result of survey responses and a literature review:

1. Resident relations.
2. Resident services.
3. Health.
4. Administration.
5. Community relations and services.

1. Resident Relations

Relationships that occur in assisted living among residents, family, and staff should be supported and encouraged. Good relationships require that the manager know residents well, understand their needs, and act to satisfy them in a way described by Terry Klaassen as "nurturing their spirit." Staff members should care for residents as if they were family members. Policies should encourage the involvement and integration of families in care decisions and service provision. Familial involvement complements what staff can do to provide for the needs of each resident.

2. Resident Services

Resident services involve the activities and care provided to residents. These should preserve dignity and privacy, provide freedom to make choices, enhance independence, and celebrate diversity and individuality.

The highest level of residents' participation in meeting their own needs should also be encouraged. A critical component of assisted living is the creation of an environment that encourages residents to make their own choices and exercise their abilities.

3. Health

Although staff members in assisted living facilities are generally not responsible for providing twenty-four-hour nursing care, they should monitor resident medications, promote wellness, and assist residents in getting necessary medical attention. A pro-active approach can be encouraged by sharing

FIGURE 4.3. *Case assessment files are kept in a central location for easy staff access:* Staff at Park Place, in Portland, OR, keep extensive notes on each resident's chronic health conditions.

the care plan with the resident and his or her family. Involving residents in their own care stimulates a sense of responsibility.

Assisted living facilities that are part of a continuing-care campus are well prepared to provide residents with needed medical services. However, free-standing facilities have improved access to medical services by working with community-based service providers to ensure that residents receive the medical care they need. Access to appropriate health care services is of primary importance in averting institutionalization.

Regulations often limit the medical services that assisted living staff can provide. However, good managers should be prepared to provide physicians with up-to-date reports on each resident's health status and to be familiar with community resources that can help residents and families when a medical situation arises.

4. Administration

Administration incorporates the basic functions of management—planning, organizing, coordinating, orchestrating, and evaluating. In assisted living, the management team must understand the special needs of its residents and be able to assist them in utilizing resources in the facility and community. Through effective administrative skills the management team can empower its residents to maximize their independence and quality of life. Because the administrator is the initial point of reference for new and potential residents, he or she can inspire a nurturing self-help philosophy that encourages residents, their families, and staff to cooperate.

5. Community Relations and Services

Good community relations promote a positive public image of the facility and are a valuable marketing tool. Ideally, the community and the facility should be resources for one another. Most important, ties with the community prompt residents to continue to be a part of the outside world. When staff and residents communicate with community organizations and individuals, everyone's quality of life is enhanced. A good community services plan involves an active exchange between the project and the community, with services made available to both the community and the residents.

Management Innovations and Exploration

Within the five categories of management practice, the following fourteen management directives further detail comprehensive management philosophy. Although a few of the surveyed facilities have developed professional management approaches using research findings described in the literature, most were established as a result of trial and error. The management directives follow.

1. Provide residents with a sense of home and community.
2. Involve families in residents' lives.
3. Allow residents to take an active role in decision making.
4. Provide activities that stimulate the mind and body.
5. Provide opportunities for volunteering and interdependence.
6. Inspire individuality and independence.
7. Provide a nutritional and socially satisfying experience.
8. Assure quality care by monitoring health status.
9. Focus on restorative health and therapy.
10. Provide a home for those with dementia.
11. Support and nurture the care-giving staff.
12. Improve resident care through applications of technology.
13. Provide educational exchanges with the community.
14. Provide service exchanges with the community.

1. Provide Residents with a Sense of Home and Community

Assisted living housing is unique in that it has great potential to provide residents with a supportive environment that also encompasses a sense of community and belonging. At the same time, it can provide residents with a place where privacy is respected and residents can be free from observation and unwelcome intrusion. However, because assisted living is for older frail persons, it can be perceived as an institutional environment and not a home-like residence.

FIGURE **4.4.** *This wrap-around exterior porch is a popular place for residents to sit:* The residential character of the Elder-Homestead in Minnetonka, MN benefits from this design feature.

Continuity in Life-Style. Assisted living environments are increasingly taking the view that a resident's initial move is the beginning of a growth cycle that is natural and positive. An example of this positive philosophy can be found at Valle Verde in Santa Barbara, California, which stresses that residents change their address, not their life-style. Life-style includes maintaining stable family relationships and friendships that are important throughout life. Good personal relationships with other residents make residents feel at home. Only when they feel loved by family and friends and accepted by their peers will they consider this housing arrangement their home.

Adjusting to a New Environment. A resident's move to assisted living may be caused by frailty; however, assistance in the activities of daily living should not be the only focus of resident interaction. Part of the staff's responsibility is to help each new resident react to the new environment as an evolution in life rather than as a foreign or frightening experience.

When residents move into assisted living they give up the familiarity of their home and neighborhood, many of their possessions, and some independence. For many residents, moving into an assisted living facility is not a welcome choice. The move is often prompted by a physician who consults with the family. In such cases residents are likely to feel powerless, frustrated, and abandoned. Many will perceive the facility as a prison without bars. This challenges management and family care givers to overcome these feelings and to help residents and their family rebuild a warm relationship. Successful adjustment to a new environment requires preservation of a resident's dignity and self-worth. Sincerity in personal contact by all concerned is especially important in minimizing adjustment problems.

A welcoming party can introduce new residents (and new staff) to the assisted living community. Even flowers delivered to the new resident's room on the first day can help ease anxieties and facilitate the adjustment process.

To promote conversations, a corner of the living room can be created. This is a place set aside for residents to display their favorite photo album, a recently completed art project, or anything they are proud of and would like to share with others. Exhibiting an item here promotes social interaction and can help build a resident's confidence, especially when his or her contributions are recognized by peers and staff.

Resident Assessment. Unlike congregate housing, admission to an assisted living facility requires a more detailed understanding of resident needs and capabilities. This normally involves an intake interview that assesses resident strengths and weaknesses. Park Place, in Portland, Oregon, estimates that fifteen to twenty hours are spent with a new resident and his or her family before admittance. The intake assessment interview should review medical, functional, psychological, and social strengths and weaknesses. Based on the information collected, a care plan can be prepared that outlines the services a resident needs and how families can be involved. When reassessment occurs on a monthly or bimonthly basis, staff members can keep track of functional improvements and areas of decline. Action can be taken quickly to modify the care plan to maintain independence and maximize functioning.

A number of assisted living residences have adopted a tiered system of care provision that uses a case management approach to identify, monitor, and resolve resident problems. It is also useful for billing purposes, because residents pay only for services received. In a three-level model system, level 1 provides basic services, which typically include three meals each day, housekeeping, personal laundry, structured activities, and transportation. Residents at this level usually require fifteen to thirty minutes of staff assistance each day. At level 2, residents require more time from staff, possibly thirty to ninety minutes daily. In addition to providing level 1 services, staff

FIGURE 4.5. *Transparencies like this window wall allow residents to preview spaces before they enter them:* The added advantage is that it can also allow daylight to reach adjacent rooms.

may need to remind these residents to take their medications, as well as help them dress and bathe. Level 2 individuals may exhibit early symptoms of Alzheimer's or Parkinson's disease. At level 3, residents require more than ninety minutes of daily staff assistance. These residents may be terminally ill or may have just returned from the hospital, exhibiting problems of incontinence, dementia, or chronic disabling conditions that severely limit their functional ability. In the past such residents would have been placed in a nursing home.

As part of the intake process at Rosewood Hall in Akron, Ohio, staff members visit the prospective resident's home in the community. They help residents select special items to bring with them. The most critical factor in helping the resident decide what to bring is the personal attachment they feel for a particular item.

If there is sufficient room, some facilities may ask residents to help decorate common spaces by volunteering items they would like to have near them but don't have space for in their room. A familiar item in a shared space helps a resident to feel that the facility is home.

2. Involve Families in Residents' Lives

On the average, three-fourths of residents normally have family members with whom they communicate regularly. Family members should be an integral part of a resident's life and an important part of the social network within the facility. They may also play instrumental roles in the facility as volunteers (e.g., by helping other residents or volunteering to assist with group events).

Provide Roles for Family Members. Visiting should be like going to grandmother and grandfather's house. Staff should be trained to acknowledge the family's role in serving the well-being of the resident. Special events and regular invitations to ongoing functions can develop a well-defined role for the family. These events could include formal education seminars; peer group discussion sessions; recreational events, such as barbecues, picnics, or outings; and conferences with family members.

An interesting example of this has been developed at Bleachwood Residence and Nursing Home in Williamsville, New York, where a support group known as the Family Council has been established. Consisting of family members and friends of residents, this group has as its purpose to improve understanding and communication with staff. The input of the council directly affects planning and decision making at the facility.

Such groups as the Family Council are valuable as a vehicle for open discussion and problem resolution. They provide a way for staff and family to communicate. Special support group meetings allow communication among families. Many family members feel guilty about placing a parent in a facility, and their guilt may create tensions during visits. Support groups such as this can be valuable in easing family tensions and adjusting family members to the move.

Involving family members and friends in the resident's health care needs ensures additional support and allows staff to develop individual goals for each resident and strategies to achieve specific objectives.

Shared Facilities with Family. A separate small kitchen used for facility activities may serve as a place for families to have a private celebration, and vacant rooms may provide lodging for families visiting from out of town. Doing the laundry is a popular activity for residents and their families.

Some facilities have purposely been designed to include places for family interaction. A movie theater and a restaurant are part of Peachwood Inn's Borden Court in Rochester Hills, Michigan. They allow a family to visit and share some of the activities the resident experienced previously. Although Peachwood Inn's Borden Court has the luxury of a bigger facility and therefore has the financial and population base to support these extra amenities, smaller facilities can find ways to ensure similar feelings of family involvement. For example, the activity room may serve as a movie theater on Friday evenings or as a private dining area for special family meals.

Family Members as a Resource. Family members can also serve as resources for the facility. A family member with a special talent may be invited to conduct activities in singing, reading, theater, cooking, or crafts for residents. Family members can also be encouraged to help residents with day-to-day activities. These may include setting up medications for the week, jointly doing the laundry, taking the resident out for a meal or to a beauty salon/barber appointment, and helping with bathing and dressing. Rosewood Estate in Roseville, Minnesota, encourages family members to be informal volunteers. Family members may help other residents with chores or provide companionship to those without families nearby.

Having grandchildren come to visit can be delightful for all residents. Facilities can encourage children to visit by giving out balloons or a surprise package such as a stuffed animal, or a party hat. Watching a happy child is a source of satisfaction and can create a pleasant mood among residents. Many residents welcome an opportunity to interact with children, and the effects of a child's visit can last long after the child goes home (Green 1990).

FIGURE 4.6. *Doing laundry is a simple activity older residents and family members can share:* At Rackleff House in Canby, OR, family members are encouraged to view this task as an opportunity for communication.

3. Allow Residents to Take an Active Role in Decision Making

Giving residents a voice in the community fosters good relations with management and inspires the residents to feel a sense of control. Although there is a great need for professionals in the assisted living industry to share ideas, it is also important to listen to residents and family members.

Providing freedom to choose among many options encourages independence and maintains a resident's sense of internal control and competence. Management staff must be creative in negotiating with residents on controversial issues, especially those that involve traditional life patterns. Policies and procedures should not dictate a single life-style nor should the life-style be driven by a therapeutic ideal. Guidelines should be available for framing reasonable resident options and alternatives.

Open Management. Management should be open to residents' suggestions and complaints. Comments from residents and their families should never be ignored. Such feedback should be treated as a measure of management effectiveness and an opportunity to recognize changes necessary for improving a facility. At the Sunrise corporate headquarters, dozens of letters from the families and friends of residents have been framed and mounted in a symbolic gesture that emphasizes the importance top management places on effective feedback.

Sunrise Retirement Home in Oakton, Virginia, conducts exit interviews with family members of residents. The interview consists of seven to ten questions and is conducted over the phone. The interviewer asks family members to assess the services and care residents receive at the facility. This also provides an opportunity for family members to ask questions. These conversations are helpful in identifying weaknesses and strengths within a facility. They also help management identify good employees who can be rewarded with a compliment, promotion, or raise.

Integrated Health Services (I.H.S.) operates about six thousand beds of subacute care, rehabilitation, assisted living, and nursing care in sixteen states. I.H.S. is customer oriented and encourages residents to take an active role in management. An 800 number is available for residents, family, and staff to comment about any aspect of any facility. The calls are viewed as a constructive and positive process, not as a negative, fault-finding action.

I.H.S. also surveys its residents regularly about their satisfaction with the facility and services. It recognizes the importance of incorporating resident feedback into its operating philosophy and takes cues from residents when making revisions. I.H.S. relies on residents' comments to mold the services it provides and refine its assisted living philosophy.

Resident Roles. In a group setting, residents are likely to take on responsibilities and roles that help shape the spirit of the facility. Welch, Parker, and Zeisel, in *Independence Through Interdependence* (1984), identify eight resident roles commonly found in congregate settings. Although assisted living residents are more frail and therefore less likely to be as active, similar roles are likely to appear in assisted living settings. Roles include the following:

- *Caretakers* actively help other residents with their daily routine. Examples include a wheelchair-bound resident who notifies staff when a disoriented resident wanders out of the room or a resident who reminds a friend to take his or her medications.
- *Informants* spend time outside the facility and bring back information from the community. They also share facility news with outsiders. They provide a positive image of the facility and may help

dismiss some of the stereotypes associated with the facility and its residents.

- *Storytellers* make an effort to talk to everyone and focus on sharing stories with others. Stories may relate to things happening outside the facility or to a personal experience. These residents offer companionship to other residents.
- *Rulemakers* are the politicians of the facility. They take the responsibility of getting involved in making facility rules. Some rulemakers may have a dominant personality, which may intimidate other residents. However, when their energies are channeled in a positive way, they can help promote a positive attitude in the facility.
- *Organizers* make sure nobody gets left out of a group event. They make sure everyone gets to meetings and remind others of upcoming events.
- *Role models* inspire other residents by their optimism, manner, and attitude. They encourage other residents to reach their optimal level of participation.
- *Delegates* are active in bringing group complaints to the manager's attention. They are valuable because some residents are afraid to voice specific concerns.
- *Balancers* are residents who communicate well with others and are good problem solvers. Their personality calms others and reduces conflict.

By recognizing the roles that residents naturally exhibit, managers can encourage residents to participate in activities that complement their skills, abilities, and personalities. For example, a resident role model may be asked to be part of the welcoming committee. The role model can meet new residents and their families while answering any questions they have that can help them adjust to the move. The social context of the setting can be strengthened by utilizing residents effectively.

Communication Tools. Common but effective staff and resident communication tools include bulletin boards, resident councils, and newsletters. Bulletin boards at various locations are useful in posting newsletters, calendars of events, menus, emergency procedures, and special announcements.

Most assisted living facilities produce their own newsletters and calendars of events. Along with the resident council, the newsletter can be used as an effective communication tool and one that builds a sense of pride

FIGURE 4.7. *Furniture contributed by residents is used in public areas:* This practice is encouraged at Elder-Homestead and has resulted in common spaces that have a varied and unique appearance.

among participants. Depending on the interests of the residents, some may volunteer to take charge of a resident column (a section written by residents) or may publish the newsletter themselves.

Providing residents with an opportunity to express their ideas, fears, and hopes through a newsletter may be therapeutic. Residents may also attain a new level of awareness of themselves and their neighbors. For those who have problems holding a pen or reading, contributions may be dictated.

Resident councils provide an effective way for residents to meet for discussions and make recommendations regarding facility policies, programs, services, and so on. Many residents welcome the opportunity to participate in self-governance and feel productive and valuable within the community. Participation allows residents a way to interact with their peers and an opportunity to practice old skills and develop new talents.

4. Provide Activities That Stimulate the Mind and Body

As the assisted living development becomes the resident's home and community, his or her world' may become smaller. Meaningful activities expand horizons; challenge the mind, body, and intellect; provide a way to mitigate loneliness and depression; and encourage independence and individuality. Interesting classes for residents provide a way to structure time and present opportunities for residents to interact and develop friendships.

Residents may view themselves more positively when they take control of their time and take steps to improve themselves. The key to designing popular activities at a facility is to tap the interest of residents. A poll may be taken periodically to identify salient interests. A task force made up of residents may be formed to help decide what activities should be offered. Residents rarely participate in all activities, since interests do vary; therefore offering a variety of activities is the key to success.

Although most residents will be frail and some may suffer from dementia, others will be mentally alert and physically strong enough to participate in trips outside the facility. The challenge for the staff is to provide activities that are appropriate and stimulating to residents of varying abilities.

Interpersonal Relations. Activities that promote self-expression help residents relate positively to those around them. Humor and enjoyment are critical to an environment that is conducive to positive interaction. Smiling, laughing, being amused, and feeling happy help friendships to develop and strengthen existing relationships. For example, music and singing can create a cheerful mood within the facility, since familiar music allows residents to reminisce and may create an environment conducive to socializing. The appreciation and understanding of music are often unaffected by dementia and thus can appeal to a broad range of residents.

The Use of Animals. Assisted living facilities use animals in various ways to help stimulate, relax, and entertain residents. Animals can also provide an air of normalcy, reinforcing the idea of a homelike environment. Many facilities bring in pets regularly for residents to enjoy. A few have opted to have a resident facility pet, usually a dog. A growing trend among social workers and recreational, physical, and occupational therapists is to use an-

FIGURE 4.8. *Small mammals are kept in elevated stands on the enclosed porch:* The Sunrise at Frederick, MD, is experimenting with a range of small animals they keep in this visible, well ventilated location.

imals to facilitate interactions and to assist in therapeutic treatment. Residents, many of whom were pet owners, often spend hours petting or watching the animals.

An article in the newsletter of the Just Like Home facility in Bradenton, Florida, reported that "Kai watching" has become one of the main attractions at the facility. Kai is a Jack Russell terrier who was brought into the facility on a trial basis. There were concerns initially about whether he would bark too much or cause accidents as he dashed around. None of these concerns seems to have materialized, and residents now view him as part of their extended family.

Animals are nonjudgmental, loyal, and supportive. They also provide unconditional affection and help residents reach an optimal level of relaxation. Stroking an animal or watching it play is pleasant for most. Animals help focus attention on the positive, thus replacing negative feelings. Not only do residents benefit from the presence of an animal, but staff and families find comfort in them as well. The Sunrise at Frederick, Maryland, has constructed pet cages on raised platforms and placed them on the enclosed porch, where ventilation is readily available and sunlight is plentiful. The Sunrise experience has shown small mammals to be most effective with dementia residents, who seem highly responsive to interaction and are often independently attracted to pets. More research with a range of animals and techniques seems warranted, given the positive feedback from the anecdotal data of facilities we surveyed.

Personal Development. Personal development relates to intellectual achievement, self-expression, useful activity, and personal awareness of dignity, independence, and self-worth. Many creative ways to promote personal development exist in an assisted living setting. Residents at Plymouth Village in Redlands, California, bury a time capsule each year. They write predictions of future events and select items that symbolize current times. This type of activity stimulates thought and encourages creativity. It also gives residents an opportunity to share their ideas, tell a story, or attach a special item.

Residents can be encouraged to explore special interests they never had time to pursue before retirement. Depending on their capabilities, these new hobbies can range widely in difficulty. Based on resident interests, needs, and capabilities, Sunrise Retirement Home tailors activities to meet individual needs. Instead of having a few activities that meet the needs of all residents, Sunrise offers a variety of different activities with the expectation that only five to ten residents will choose to participate in any one event. The importance of activities lies in the meaning and level of satisfaction each activity provides for residents. A new hobby may be as simple as listening to classical music, or it may involve painting, writing, gardening, or a more physical activity. The goal of this approach is to have residents nurture past interests and continue to feel value and purpose in life.

Activities may also incorporate one-on-one tasks where staff members work directly with residents. Personalized activity programs can be identified during resident assessments and may be incorporated into the daily care routine of a resident.

By working with residents, staff members may find that one was an avid letter writer but can no longer hold a pen because of arthritis. Part of the individual activity for this person may be to identify new pen pals or to dictate letters. It should also include assistance in using a tape recorder to enable sending a "talking letter" to pen pals.

A special audio tape or video can be made by the family to provide sensory stimulation for confused or disoriented residents. The personalized audio tape may include family members talking to the resident, singing or playing an instrument, or a family pet barking or meowing. A video can capture almost anything and can range from a family Thanksgiving dinner to a grandchild's wedding ceremony and reception.

Some activities require little staff supervision. For example, a quilting or puzzle table can be used at almost any time and provides participating residents with social opportunities as well as a challenging problem.

Because women make up the majority of assisted living residents, activities may inadvertently cater more to their preferences, in which case men may feel out of place. Special activities may be considered for men. At Plymouth Village in Redlands, California, male residents periodically go out for beer and pizza.

FIGURE 4.9. *Farmer's Market display goods in project atrium:* Each week a local merchant visits this project to sell fresh fruit and vegetables.

Spiritual and Transcendental. Many people become introspective and philosophical and take time to evaluate their lives as they grow older. They also are more inclined to think of what will happen to them after death. Managers should first encourage residents to seek fellowship, churches, temples, and synagogues outside the facility. However, residents should be provided with options at the facility as well. Most assisted living facilities provide spiritual activities for residents, and because of their potential popularity, management may consider expanding these. For example, a daily prayer session or Bible study may be implemented. Spiritual and transcendental activities such as fellowship, religious study, meditation, and hymn singing can also be included.

5. Provide Opportunities for Volunteering and Interdependence

In *Serving the Ageless Market: Strategies for Selling to the Fifty-plus Market,* David Wolfe identifies altruism as one of the keys to selling products to older people. Older customers tend to respond favorably to messages that emphasize their role as unselfish and interested in the welfare of others. A sense of altruism is especially important for assisted living residents. Many feel a void because they are no longer in a working environment or nurturing role.

According to Erik Erickson's seventh stage of psychosocial development (approximately after middle age), adults focus on giving back to the community—altruism. They need and want a productive role, which may be expressed in public service, creative endeavors, or teaching. Twenty-three residents participating voluntarily in a work therapy program at the Wisconsin Veterans' Home were interviewed regarding their perceptions of the program. Administered by a work therapy coordinator, goals of the program included increasing self-esteem and helping residents improve their physical capabilities. Work assignments varied and were assigned according to resident ability; they included mopping, sweeping, teaching crafts, and clerical work. Ninety percent of those interviewed reported an increase in their self-esteem as a result of having a job. Eighty percent felt their work was important (Voeks and Drinka 1990).

Assign Roles and Work Tasks. Residents in an assisted living facility can be assigned tasks they are capable of performing and will enjoy. One may help pass out mail while another opens curtains in the morning or waters indoor plants. Residents may be asked to raise the American flag every

FIGURE 4.10. *Informal helping exchanges provide satisfaction to the giver and the receiver:* At the Captain Eldridge Congregate House "extended-family relationships" characterize how residents care for one another.

morning and take it down at night, help with gardening, arrange flowers, or set the dinner table. They can also provide valuable services for the community. Programs such as Foster Grandparents allow seniors to be a friend and role model to youths at risk. At Carewest Convalescent Home in Orange County, California, resident volunteers who are physically and cognitively able act as counselors and role models to young offenders (Jarvis 1989).

Residents of the Home, in Auburn, New York, belong to the Retired Senior Volunteer Program (RSVP). Through RSVP they volunteer to compile newsletters for other agencies, act as foster grandparents for disabled children, and conduct a literacy program. Although the majority of assisted living residents will probably not be involved in the typical work force, those residents who are capable can benefit from volunteer programs. Foster Grandparents usually reimburses transportation expenses and provides participants with an annual physical exam and stipend.

For low-functioning residents, a food-tasting committee may be developed. Members of the tasting committee vote on menus and critique new dishes. Residents at Elder Homestead in Minnetonka, Minnesota, share favorite recipes with a story or history. Selected dishes are served to all residents and the contributing resident is recognized.

Some residential outreach programs may be more seasonal. For example, residents of Rosewood Hall in Akron, Ohio, participated in decorating a Christmas tree that was auctioned for $400. The proceeds were then donated to a local Children's Hospital.

6. Inspire Individuality and Independence

Independence entails the ability to make one's own choices and retain a sense of control over one's life. Choice and control are powerful psychosocial forces that affect self-esteem and life satisfaction. Assisted living facilities should make needed services available to residents while taking precautions against overprotecting them.

Allowing residents to take risks and to behave in an unhealthy way is difficult for clinically trained personnel. However, the essence of institutionalization centers on controlling and modifying behaviors so as to make them conform with established norms. In assisted living this freedom is complicated by group norms established for resident behavior. It is important to allow older residents to continue habits like smoking, eating inappropriate foods, and violating dietary regimens if they insist on these behaviors once they have been apprised of their negative consequences. However, it is important to avoid any negative effects (like secondary smoke) these habits may have on other residents.

Also, allowing a resident to stay in his or her room, take a meal alone, or stay in pajamas for most of the day ought to be possible in any setting. Regimenting behavior ignores the potential of individual expression, which is the essence of the human condition and underlies the rich diversity represented by the human race. Reconciling individual desires within the context of a group living environment may be difficult and complicated, but it is necessary. A management philosophy that allows residents to exercise control over their situation reduces dependence on family members or friends.

Rosewood Estate in Roseville, Minnesota, gives residents an opportunity to "buy" services in fifteen-minute increments. These services include bathing, dressing and grooming, grocery shopping, and transportation. By unbundling services, residents and family members are given added incentives to be more self-sufficient. This encourages residents to be responsible for helping themselves and their friends and spurs families to be more involved in the care of their relative.

Life-long Independence. Success in maintaining independence and preserving dignity allows residents to be supported through increasing levels of dependence. The philosophy of assisted living focuses on avoiding institutionalization so that residents can stay in a homelike environment typical of traditional cultural patterns until their death. Sunrise Retirement Homes considers this an indication of success, since institutionalization is avoided.

A number of assisted living facilities encourage residents who are able to go home once they learn how to take better care of themselves. For example, with proper nutrition and a more structured regimen, once confused residents may be able to take care of themselves at home or in a less restrictive environment. Staff may help choose the right foods or locate services such as meals-on-wheels to remedy the problem that originally brought these residents into the facility.

Transportation is a valuable service, for it encourages residents to maintain continuity with the outside world and to continue to participate in activities they enjoyed before entering assisted living. The availability of transportation encourages trips to beauty salons, church services, and other familiar places without residents having to rely on family or friends.

Technology. It is sometimes difficult to provide independence and privacy when a facility is also responsible for the well-being of a resident. The "flipper" system at the King's Crown at Shell Point Village in Fort Myers, Florida, works well to maintain privacy while informing staff of each resident's status. Night staff place a flipper on each apartment door in an up position between 3 and 4 A.M. The flipper is designed to drop to the down position as soon as the door opens and residents leave their rooms for breakfast. If it is still in the up position at 10 A.M., the day aide knocks to check on the resident. If there is no answer the manager or nurse uses the master key to check to see if the resident has overslept or is in need of assistance.

7. Provide a Nutritional and Socially Satisfying Dining Experience

Meals are important for residents in an assisted living facility. They not only provide residents with nutritional requirements, but also offer an opportunity for social interaction and a time to make decisions. Dining is a consistent, regularly scheduled activity that can be anticipated by dressing up if the occasion warrants it.

Nutrition. An adequate diet helps prevent some disorders, provides energy that aids in the growth and repair of tissues, regulates the body's elimination of waste, and stimulates the appetite. Proper nutrition is a major component of good health at all ages. Malnutrition can be a problem among the elderly. Nursing home studies have shown residents often suffer from some degree of malnutrition. Assisted living facilities are not immune.

Each resident has a set of nutritional requirements that may differ from those of other residents of the same age, sex, or ethnic group. These requirements should therefore be assessed upon admission to an assisted living facility and updated as part of a frequent monitoring plan. Changing medication regimens or pathological conditions must also be considered in a comprehensive dietary plan.

Although it may sometimes be a challenge, it is the responsibility of the dietary team to provide residents with a menu that meets their nutritional requirements as well as personal preferences. If there are minority residents, meals should meet cultural and traditional expectations. Special dishes for holidays should be included. When a resident is unwilling to eat properly or to eat enough, the manager and dietary team need to work creatively with the resident to solve the problem.

Dining Experience. The dining experience itself is valuable for residents and gives them an opportunity to interact. To ensure resident satisfaction, managers and the dietary team can join residents during meals. The staff should not only taste the food, but also evaluate the dining room ambience and talk with residents to ensure that they enjoy their dining experience. The dining room must feel like a family restaurant. Evaluations should consider the service, the feelings of camaraderie between residents and staff, and the presentation of food. A deteriorating sense of smell; less sensitive, aging tastebuds; and the side effects of medication make the presentation of food especially important. Moreover, cooking smells reinforce a homelike feeling and act as a reminder that meals are imminent.

Respect Resident Privacy. Some residents may have life-long eating habits and may not want to take all meals in the dining room. Early risers may not want to wait until 8:00 or 9:00 for breakfast. Others may want to enjoy a leisurely morning and have breakfast in their room. Although residents should be encouraged to eat with others, their wish to have some meals alone should be respected. Palm Crest in Long Beach, California, serves three meals and two snacks each day, with a continental breakfast delivered to the resident's room every morning. Rosewood Estate in Roseville, Minnesota, estimates that 10 to 15 percent of residents take breakfast in their rooms.

A facility may also consider staggered mealtimes, so that residents can

FIGURE **4.11.** *Private dining room facilities allow residents to host family functions:* At the Sunrise at Fairfax, VA, birthday parties are popular family events.

eat in convenient shifts. Such a schedule accommodates resident preferences better and creates a more intimate feeling because a smaller number of residents eat at one time.

8. Assure Quality Care by Monitoring Health Status

The resident care plan is a communication tool for the facility staff. A well-thought-out and well-written plan will utilize different services to meet a resident's unique needs.

The patient care plan starts at admission. During the intake process a complete assessment of the resident is made, from which specific objectives are set. Objectives should be measurable and attainable. For example, one objective for an incontinent resident would be to increase continence. The aim could be to reduce the number of "accidents" gradually over a six-month period, at which time the resident might be able to control bowel or bladder problems.

A resident care plan also specifies the role and responsibility of each participant, including the resident, family members, medical personnel, and

FIGURE 4.12. *Pharmaceuticals, diagnostic equipment and resident health care records are kept in a central location:* Sunrise facilities use bubble medicine packaging to reduce errors and streamline operations.

personal care aides. Success in this endeavor depends on the staff building positive and personal relationships through encouragement. In the facilities of the Sunrise Retirement Homes, staff members take responsibility for knowing each resident's background and preferences (e.g., how they like their coffee or tea).

All staff members informally monitor resident health by recognizing subtle changes in behavior and communicating them to the appropriate person. This promotes an attitude of personal caring that increases a resident's self-worth and recognizes individuality. With a weekly review of each resident, a slight irregularity can be checked and a medical crisis avoided.

Multidisciplinary Approach. Many assisted living facilities have adopted a multidisciplinary approach to resident care plans. An example is the Individualized Functional Assessment Scale (IFAS) used by the Judson Retirement Community in Cleveland, Ohio. The IFAS serves as a tool in making decisions about a resident's changing level of care.

The IFAS assesses a resident's level of independence in managing Activities of Daily Living (ADL) and Instrumental Activities of Daily Living (IADL). Behavior, physical health, mental health, motivation, and social relationships are also assessed by staff members who have been caring for the resident. Residents are also evaluated on the basis of input from key staff. During staff meetings, information is shared and the staff "brainstorm" the best way to help the resident maintain a high level of independent functioning. The more assistance required, the higher the resident's IFAS score. Scores are given for the following assessment areas:
ADLs:

> Ability to move about the environment independently.
> Ability to eat independently.
> Ability to maintain personal hygiene.
> Ability to dress independently and appropriately.
> Ability to care for toileting needs.

IADLs:

> Ability to use the telephone.
> Ability to shop.
> Ability to prepare meals.
> Ability to participate in housekeeping.
> Ability to do laundry.

Ability to provide transportation.
Ability to take responsibility for medication.
Ability to manage personal finances.

Health:

Stability of health.
Staff time required to manage health care problems.

Mental health:

Ability to solve problems.
Ability to function independently in managing day-to-day tasks, taking into account judgment, orientation, and memory.

Behavior:

Amount of staff time required to manage residents' problems.
Self-inflicted resident stress.
Stress on staff.
Stress on others (i.e., family, other residents).

Motivation:

Cooperative attitude.
Passive attitude.
Uncooperative attitude.

Two staff members may give a resident different scores. Staff with varying training and experience may also interpret the same resident differently. However, a tool like the IFAS provides a more dependable basis for comparison.

9. Focus on Restorative Health and Therapy

Forestalling institutionalization or avoiding it altogether requires careful attention to the physical and ambulatory needs of residents. If residents are left to deteriorate, they may soon need to be moved to a nursing home. Frailty is often accepted as a part of aging, but it often results from inactivity. Rehabilitation differs from restorative therapy in that it involves occupational, physical, recreational, and speech therapies delivered independently, whereas restorative therapy is interdisciplinary, using a team approach that coordinates various treatments.

Make'Exercise Fun and Positive. An exercise program oriented toward varying levels of fitness, preservation of muscle strength, enhancing ambulatory capabilities, and improving aerobic capacity should be available. Teaching residents to be aware and responsible for their own self-care needs is essential. Therapy and exercise can be disguised as a pleasant recreational diversion, since exercise may carry a stigma. Older women who were taught that it is unladylike to sweat may also need the attention of staff members, who can creatively suggest ways in which women can find a suitable activity while respecting their beliefs. Exercise can become a life-style habit, one as simple as walking up and down stairs to dinner. Most important in promoting exercise for seniors is ensuring that it occurs regularly.

A restorative health program organized and administered by a physical therapist, or aide, is appropriate as part of the resident care plan for each resident whose ambulatory needs require it. Such a wellness program initiated four years ago at Mt. San Antonio Gardens' Oak Lodge in Pomona, California, focuses on the positive aspects of aging. The program empowers and motivates residents to function at their optimal level. Those who participate in it become role models to others by demonstrating that no one is too old or too disabled to strive for a healthier life-style and that improvement is possible at all levels.

The objectives of the wellness program are as follows:

1. To assure that each resident has the appropriate assistive devices for ambulation and other activities of daily living.
2. To design individual and group programs that build strength, endurance, flexibility, balance, coordination, and self-confidence.
3. To prevent premature admission to the skilled nursing facility.
4. To provide for continuity of care and a smooth transition from acute hospitalization and/or skilled nursing facility stays back to the assisted living facility.

A consulting physical therapist at Mt. San Antonio gardens screens all new residents, determines their rehabilitation needs, and recommends activities. Some residents perform daily chair exercises. Many participate in an individualized exercise program conducted by a physical therapy aide. Exercise mats, weight-lifting equipment, parallel bars, stationary bicycles, and various other equipment are located in a multipurpose activity room accessible to all residents.

Aquatic Exercise. When implemented by a well-trained staff, an aquatic therapy program can be a safe and effective way for residents to participate

FIGURE 4.13. *Exercise equipment for the specific physiological requirements of the older person is more available today:* This gym at Leisure World in Laguna Hills, CA, has an exercise physiologist on staff.

in an exercise program. The buoyancy of water supports the body and protects the bones, joints, and muscles. Moreover, water offers resistance, which means that muscles work harder than they do normally, thereby providing exercise. The effects of moving water are similar to those in pushing a weight, for movement becomes harder with increased speed. This provides the resistance needed to strengthen muscles without the strain that regular weights may cause.

Aquatic exercise can especially help residents with arthritis, strokes, joint replacements, and Parkinson's disease. Such residents can find other types of exercise difficult or impossible because of tenderness in the joints or paralysis. Aquatic exercise can also be a lot of fun. Some residents who are confined to a wheelchair may find they move more freely in water. Weekly water exercise classes are held in a heated pool at The Hampton at Post Oak in Houston, Texas. The program, led by a certified water exercise instructor, grew to include fifteen full-time participants within six months.

Depth. The Day Enrichment Program Toward Health (DEPTH) grew out of a need to develop a program for the physically frail who are still socially and mentally alert. It is offered by Valle Verde in Santa Barbara, California,

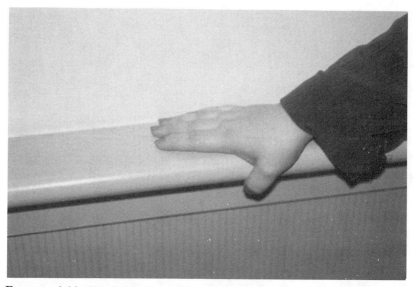

FIGURE 4.14. *Hand rails disguised as chair rails are successful at Sunrise facilities:* These are 3.5 inches wide and are located on both sides of a relatively narrow corridor.

through a thirteen-week summer program for residents and the community. DEPTH promotes wellness, socialization, and support group experiences through health, educational, and physical activities. Classes include exercise, nutrition, memory enhancement, growth through change and loss, communication skills, the proper use of medication, speech therapy, and games.

10. Provide a Home to Those with Dementia

Residents with dementia may exhibit difficult behavior. For example, a confused resident may become violent and uncooperative when she does not understand how her environment is changing. In the past, institutionalization was almost the only option for such a person. However, with creative methods and interventions and with a well-trained staff, those with dementia can live comfortably and with minimal problems in assisted living.

Family and Friends. Kingsley Manor in Los Angeles, California, has set aside one wing of thirteen units for residents with Alzheimer's disease or

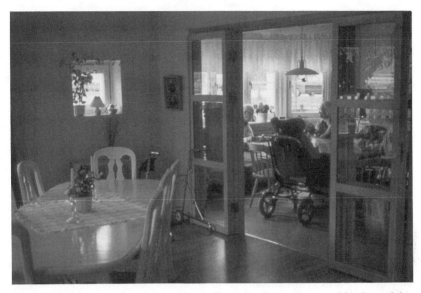

FIGURE **4.15.** *Transparent window walls to the dining room and kitchen of this group home cue residents with memory problems:* They can see into the room and remember the destination they are headed toward.

other cognitive impairments. Although residents in this wing continue to be a part of the Kingsley community, they receive additional support. Family and friends are asked to bring personal items that the residents were familiar with prior to the onset of their mental deterioration.

Staff members ask questions about family pictures to help orient residents and encourage them to make choices by asking them what they would like to wear. A name plate beside each door helps residents find their rooms. Finally, doors are decorated with a wreath, picture, or small American flag to assist residents in finding their room.

In advanced stages, when decision making becomes more difficult and residents are most vulnerable to institutionalization, Sunrise Retirement Home care givers provide additional support to minimize the impact of difficult decisions. For example, clothing for each day of the week is assembled in advance and identified by the day of the week it will be worn. Extra clothes are kept in a separate place to minimize confusion.

Popular Activities. A few years ago gerontology graduate students from the University of Southern California residing at Kingsley Manor's campus surveyed Alzheimer residents about the activities they enjoyed most. Bingo with prizes, exercise classes, Bible classes, and reading for discussion were and continue to be popular. The Bible class with staff-encouraged discussion and participation is also enjoyed by some high-competency residents.

The Alzheimer's Care Center in Gardiner, Maine, is an assisted living facility catering only to the mentally frail. Part of its therapy is to involve residents in familiar activities. For example, one of the center's residents is a former teacher. During a group discussion led by staff, the resident stands next to the blackboard and writes words that fellow residents call out. Writing on the board is a task that she has performed countless times and that she still does well. Another resident, a former homemaker, enjoys dusting and cleaning up after meals. Performing even a simple task to help out brings satisfaction to residents and allows them to cope better during the day. By using past stimuli as a guide, staff members work to provide an environment that enhances existing resident skills. They have found that many residents who play a musical instrument can still do so as well as they did in the past. Residents also go on frequent field trips that have included apple picking, maple sugaring, county fairs, and the circus.

Technology. One important issue in managing Alzheimer's residents is their potential to wander. The Praxis Alzheimer Facility in Easton, Pennsylvania, a nursing home, solved this concern by an electronic control system called Stroll-Control that helps keep residents in the building. The device is a wristband for residents that incorporates a microcircuit and an electromagnetic door lock that is activated when residents approach the door.

This system allows staff and family to walk freely through the doors. Also, it does not agitate residents with a loud alarm. Normally, when residents find the door locked, they lose interest and move on to another part of the room. The Stroll-Control system is automatically deactivated when the fire alarm is set and can be turned off manually from the nurses' station or at the door itself.

11. Support and Nurture the Care-Giving Staff

In a business where staff turnover is high, administration must try to encourage employees to stay. Turnover creates a number of problems. It costs money to replace an employee, and training is time-consuming. But most important, turnover disrupts the stability of the facility, making it difficult for residents to build continuity and friendship with staff members.

FIGURE 4.16. *The French "serre" is a glass enclosed balcony that can be used as an interior room or a balcony:* In this project, residents have carpeted the floor and furnished it as a reading room.

Make Staff Feel Important. Staff members are critical in carrying out the objectives of an assisted living program and should feel good about what they do. They must also know, understand, and believe in the philosophy of the facility. In fact, the success of any assisted living arrangement depends on maintaining a quality care-giving staff.

Pretraining is a valuable way for a new employee to feel welcome and competent at a new job. Ongoing training is also essential in reviewing and enhancing old skills and in learning new ones.

Like many other businesses, a number of assisted living facilities encourage employees to take courses outside the facility. Many administrators recognize that education benefits both the staff member and the facility and therefore offer scholarships. I.H.S. has a stock option plan for all staff members that allows them to own a part of the company.

Most of the staff at the Alzheimer's Care Center in Gardiner, Maine, have no previous experience. This allows trainers to "mold" staff members and to "unteach" previous work habits learned in a nursing facility. Initial training lasts for two weeks. Ongoing in-service training is provided to fine-tune skills, and tuition assistance is available for those who want additional certification. This fosters the feeling that staff members are important; as a result, they feel part of a special project.

Unpredictable intermittent reinforcement is a powerful psychological device for encouraging behavioral change. Sunrise uses a version of this in a staff incentive program that is reported to be highly successful. An individual unknown to the staff enters the building. The first staff member who smiles and greets that person is given two theater tickets. The "Sunrise smile" program, as it is called, was devised as an incentive to promote a positive show of affection between the staff and people entering a Sunrise home. Incentives of this sort reinforce attitudes about behavior with rewards that recognize compliance.

Bob Elkins, of Integrated Health Services, stresses the importance of having a distinct vision of the facility through a statement of values embraced by management and staff. A number of managers have found that experienced staff members often have a "nursing home philosophy" that is hard to overcome. They are typically more likely to perform tasks for residents than to challenge them to attempt the tasks themselves. Because assisted living is a new industry, there are few experienced aides and therapists with effective problem-solving techniques.

Building an effective company and developing a strong culture within the facility are important and require that staff members operate as a team.

Recommit Staff to High Standards. Many facilities are starting to stress the importance of involving employees in quality control. Hillhaven Corporation has implemented an all-encompassing quality approach for its fifty-five western nursing facilities that involves all categories of employees from housekeeping staff to administrators.

The program, Care Excellence, commits employees to high standards of patient care and promotes nine standards developed through surveys of residents, families, employees, physicians, and discharge planners. The standards are as follows:

1. Provide a caring and well-trained professional staff.
2. Be courteous and attentive to everyone's needs.
3. Provide a pleasant and safe living environment.
4. Honor each resident's right to be treated with dignity and respect.
5. Offer each resident the opportunity to continue a normal lifestyle.
6. Help residents achieve their highest level of independence.
7. Ensure residents' comfort and well-being and help them to look their best.
8. Enhance the dining experience of each resident.
9. Work together to provide the best medical programs and the finest health care services.

Monthly sessions focus on one of the nine Care Excellence standards. Inservice sessions are about thirty-five minutes long and include role playing and group discussions. These sessions are followed within two weeks by a Team Excellence meeting that includes employees in each department. The team meeting is led by a supervisor who attends the monthly session. The meetings are short but important. All departmental staff discuss specific actions they can take to achieve the goal for the month.

12. Improve Resident Care Through Applications of Technology

Technological developments in communications and electromechanical robotic devices are quickly changing the lives of Americans, saving time, and improving the quality of life of their users. Devices such as dishwashers, microwaves, and personal computers, which were considered luxury items not long ago, are now the norm in the American household.

When technology is integrated into resident care, the goal should be to help residents remain independent and free staff time without sacrificing one-on-one interactions between staff and residents. In fact, technology should enable staff members to devote more time to the individual needs of residents. For example, the Stroll-Control system for Alzheimer residents allows them to explore their environment with little supervision and gives staff extra time to work on personal projects with individual residents. Care must also be taken to integrate technologies without taking away from the homelike environment.

FIGURE 4.17. *A two tone alarm system is wired to the telephone at Sunrise facilities:* Residents can summon staff using an emergency button or a standard call feature.

Computerization and Documentation. Resident care problems can stem from inconsistent and incomplete communications among the staff and poor documentation of what is and is not being done. Staff members collect a vast amount of information for each resident. To provide continuity of care it is important that staff members update one another on the status of each resident before each shift changes.

Discussing each resident can be time-consuming, even if comments are brief. This leads to miscommunication of residents' needs and goals. Staff members may provide services that are no longer needed while leaving out new tasks.

Staff members may feel that there is not enough time to document everything that goes on and may leave items out. Even when they do document something, it may be a week after the event. If residents' records are not updated daily, there is a greater chance of misdiagnosing a problem.

A good computer program can update a resident file and generate a daily report with assignment flow sheets that specify the roles for each staff member for that day. Assignment sheets will list the resident's needs and goals to help the staff member understand why each task is being performed. With a document in front of them, staff members can discuss specific details of a resident's status.

A computer system also has billing capability. For example, at Rosewood Estate, in Roseville, Minnesota, residents are charged for care provided, in intervals of fifteen minutes. By having the staff input information immediately into a computer system, the financial department is always current. In addition, current needs are always known and can be easily updated to reflect changing service requirements. A computer system allows departments to access the latest information on residents without the typical difficulties that can arise in a manually controlled system as a result of variations in a resident's service plan.

FIGURE 4.18. *A computer task assignment system coordinated with a lifeline emergency response system allows help to be deployed as needed:* Computer technology also facilitates billing and record keeping at Rosewood Estate.

13. Provide Educational Exchanges with the Community

An assisted living facility can provide students with a place to learn about aging and can be especially important as a laboratory for students considering a career in gerontology. The presence of students keeps residents in touch with the outside world and helps them feel like participants in the community.

Residents of the Motion Picture Country House and Hospital in Woodland Hills, California, can participate in clinical research programs sponsored by local universities. Two to four graduate students from the University of Southern California's gerontology program are provided with room and board at Kingsley Manor in Los Angeles, California, in exchange for fourteen hours of work each week. Work responsibilities range from answering telephones to assisting with activities. Others work in the marketing department, making phone calls, meeting prospects, and assisting with advertising.

The arrangements work well both for the facility and for the students, who gain practical experience as they live and work with a population that will be the focus of their career. Room and board in an area where rental rates are high is also an incentive for students. The students add a feeling of added security for residents and often enhance morale.

High School Student Exchange. Some facilities also have partnership programs with younger students. An intergenerational program at Aldersgate Village Assisted Living Center in Topeka, Kansas, matches residents with a high school junior or senior. Students are enrolled in a Parenthood Education class as part of their study of the aging process. They also participate in exercise classes, knead bread dough, and listen to residents reminisce about their earlier years. In addition, students organize a fashion show as one of their activities, modeling current fashions as well as those from the past. Students and residents often find they have a lot in common and frequently form lasting friendships.

14. Provide Service Exchanges with the Community

As the name implies, the Evergreen Hospice Center in Kirkland, Washington, provides care for the terminally ill. At the center, staff help residents maintain their dignity and comfort by offering them and their families care choices. Staff members also assist family and friends in supporting and caring for residents. Volunteers are welcomed in the facility and are an integral

FIGURE **4.19.** *Staff offices fit the residential context at Elder-Homestead:* They are located behind first-floor resident social areas.

component of the care delivery team. In return, Evergreen provides the community with seminars about death and dying and offers counseling and respite care.

Whenever possible, managers should encourage staff members from different facilities to meet to exchange ideas and information and to solve problems. Staff at Rochester Area Adult Homes and the Rochester Presbyterian Home of Rochester, New York, meet quarterly to share ideas. They jointly advertise to increase public awareness of assisted living. Residents of the facilities also participate in friendly competitions, including spelling bees, trivia challenges, volleyball, field trips, and lunches. These activities benefit residents and expand their social contacts and relationships.

To celebrate National Older American's month in May, Valle Verde in Santa Barbara, California, has a senior cook-off and open house for the community. Events include a cook-off contest for local seniors, in the categories of breads/rolls, main dishes, desserts/pastries, and "light and right" (dishes with less fat and salt). Food demonstrations by celebrity chefs and exhibits of products and services are conducted and professional music groups perform. Moreover, a *Cinco de Mayo* barbecue is available for $5. In 1993 about 1,300 people attended.

Conclusions

Managing a successful therapeutic environment involves the integration of the directives described. Underlining the management directives are fundamental philosophies that emerge and help to define a standard of assisted living. These philosophies are the following:

1. Accept the Frail Years as a Natural and Positive Component of the Life Cycle

A resident's move into an assisted living facility may be prompted by frailty and the insistence of family and/or a physician, so that residents often view the move negatively. Residents and families must recognize that assisted living offers a supportive environment that promotes independence and can increase the quality of life.

2. Allow Residents to Continue with a Familiar Life-Style

Moving into an assisted living setting does not and should not terminate relationships and ties with people outside the facility. It is important that residents continue to feel a part of the community and be able to relate to it comfortably. Residents should remain involved in community affairs by being encouraged to continue to attend church or visit beauty salons in their old neighborhoods. Within the housing, they should be allowed to continue chores they performed before they moved in.

3. Provide Residents with Opportunities for Growth

It is important for residents to have a productive and fulfilling role in the facility and external community. The time that they have can be used to master old skills and to develop new hobbies and talents. Accommodations should be made to allow residents to find activities that allow personal growth. Depending on their interests and capabilities, they should have options to work and volunteer.

4. Support and Nurture the Care-Giving Staff

The care-giving staff is crucial in ensuring that the objectives of an assisted living setting are carried out. They provide stability for residents and the foundation for a successful program. Staff must be trained and committed to quality standards. A team approach is important and should be encouraged through pride and loyalty to residents. A strong sense of professional dedication can be achieved through incentives, such as recognition awards, pay raises and bonuses, scholarships, and promotions.

5. Involve Family Members

For assisted living to succeed in providing a homelike environment for the frail elderly it must involve family members in the lives of residents. Family

FIGURE 4.20. *This strategically placed table is the 100% corner:* Located near the entrance, front desk and stair of the Argyle in Denver, CO it is heavily used throughout the day.

members must feel welcome when visiting their relatives. They should feel there is still an important place for them in a resident's life. When a family member feels uncomfortable or guilty, the staff can intervene by providing individual counseling to alleviate negative feelings. Family members can be an important resource for the facility, and some may welcome the opportunity to volunteer their time or help other residents who may not have families nearby.

6. Focus on Restorative Health and Therapy

Residents' physical and mental capabilities can be maximized through a team approach that involves staff, family members, and the resident. A well-thought-out and well-written resident-care plan will specify the role and responsibility of each participant. With regular resident reviews, staff, family, and the resident can recognize changes and communicate them to the appropriate staff person in an effort to maintain the optimum level of functioning. Staff members can motivate residents to take responsibility for their own care by providing attractive, healthy meals and making exercise enjoyable.

7. Take Advantage of New Technologies

Assisted living can greatly benefit from modern technology, which can save staff time and therefore allow more individualized attention to be given to residents. With careful planning, technology can be integrated into the facility without detracting from its homelike atmosphere. Technology can free residents from constant supervision and can make them feel more independent.

Challenges for the Future

It is an exciting time for assisted living housing. Clearly, the industry is still in its infancy. However, we can already see the potential it has to enable frail elders to live a fulfilling and dignified life in a residential environment that stresses independence.

Managing assisted living offers great challenges, as we are only beginning to define and understand effective therapeutic interventions. To ensure its success and credibility, the industry must have a resident-centered approach and strive for excellence. Practitioners must share ideas and continually seek ways to improve the quality of care, since offering quality care is the best guarantee against an increase in regulations that may deter innovation.

Disorientation, restlessness, and incontinence are no longer good enough reasons to institutionalize an older frail person. The need for residential environments that aid, assist, and enhance the lives of the mentally and physically frail will continue to grow.

5. Financing Construction and Ongoing Operations

The successful development of an assisted living project depends on the planned interaction of a combination of processes. After a market feasibility analysis confirms the need for such a project, planning, design, marketing, and management activities must follow. Existing literature generally focuses on these areas as the important elements of a successful implementation plan. Financial factors, including cost-benefit effectiveness and ongoing cost analysis, are typically not stressed. But the key vehicle for successfully implementing and operating any project is a sound financial approach. This is a component of the assisted living industry that has received little creative attention.

As a result of the changing political and economic philosophies of recent years and the number of failures in up-scale congregate housing, long-term financing has become increasingly difficult to acquire. Major considerations in the successful implementation of assisted living for the elderly must therefore include both the current financial climate and general financing trends.

Current Financial Climate

In general, the participants surveyed in our study and the trade journal literature indicate that financial institutions are somewhat cautious about investment opportunities in market rate senior housing. Investment in assisted living appears timid, although there seem to be no specific barriers that make financing insurmountable. In fact, the passage of the Omnibus Reconciliation Act of 1990 (OBRA) brought considerable renewed optimism for the funding of long-term care choices for Americans, specifically in the area of assisted living (ALFAA 1990). Through Section 4711, Congress appropriated $580 million for a Medicaid program to provide assisted living services. Congress also appropriated $100 million, through Section 4712, for a new Medicaid program to provide "community-supported living arrangements services" that include assistance in activities of daily living.

The current immaturity of the assisted living industry has fostered investor insecurity. Financial programs in real estate are often held back by the perception of high risk. In a study of the financial industry's views on senior living environments, Mark de Reus (1987) suggests that investment in assisted living involves some amount of risk . This idea emanates from four major areas of decision making that affect the success of an assisted living project:

1. Marketplace.
2. Facility design.
3. Facility management.
4. Regulations and politics.

1. Marketplace

The biggest financial concern expressed by nonprofit organizations involved in developing assisted living facilities is the nature of the investment market. Since the elderly who seek an assisted living arrangement are typically frail and vulnerable, they operate from a position of need rather than desire. Consequently, lenders appear to believe that assisted living precedes an imminent move to a nursing home. In fact, administrators actually estimated that on average a resident stayed for one and a half to three years.

Aging in Place. Participants in this study were generally committed to the concept of residents staying in assisted living until their death. However, many lenders have typically assumed that the funds of residents will dwindle quickly and that the housing arrangement (especially if it is operated by a nonprofit organization) will be left to care for an individual whose income does not cover the cost of services. For the most part this fear has proved erroneous, because assisted living has generally been developed for a market of seniors with enough income to manage their month-to-month lease obligations.

However, as the elderly become more aware of the dynamic concept of aging in place and increasingly express this as their housing preference, assisted living will compete for resources with adult day care, home health services, and other community-oriented service programs. The market for long-term care, with increasingly available options, therefore requires assisted living facilities to compete openly for residents. This competition can be expected to grow as congregate housing facilities built in the 1980s add more personal-care services and many nursing homes respond to changing market conditions by either refurbishing or converting to assisted living (Mullen 1991). Also important to remaining competitive is recognizing the need for replacing the traditional medical model of long-term care and its institutional configuration with the residential model of assisted living.

Occupancy Considerations. Unfortunately, skepticism arises from the perception that newly developed assisted living facilities may not consistently offer sufficient economic incentives to attract major investors. Occupancy rates for many assisted living facilities have thus far been little higher than those of congregate-care and continuing-care retirement communities (CCRC) (Mullen 1991). However, facilities that incorporate comprehensive and integrated market feasibility, planning, design, marketing, and management concepts in their strategy usually fill up quickly. The facilities of Sunrise Retirement Homes have frequently reached capacity in three to six months.

Regardless, lenders and investors assume that operating deficits, construction, lease-up period interest expense, and marketing costs will remain as high as those for congregate or CCRC projects. Our survey participants also expressed concern about the extended time periods spent renting or selling units and the consequent impact on carrying costs.

As a result, in the past two years, with the downtrend in the economy, we have seen investors focusing on a short-turnaround, limited investment time frame and on the need to define risk more clearly. This is especially true for wealthy overseas investors, who often look to make a substantial profit with minimum risk. Assisted living developers have consequently increased their acquisition and remodeling of existing stock; meanwhile the inventory of newly constructed buildings has declined. Until the economy stabilizes, this trend can probably be expected to continue, although new assisted living facilities will still be built.

These problems do not result from risks inherent in developing an assisted living industry. Returns on equity can be adequate for the risk assumed, but they will be realized only if assisted living facilities (newly con-

FIGURE 5.1. *Lifeline emergency response systems are increasingly being monitored by senior centers and care facilities:* This housing project in Finland monitors the 49 residents in the facility, 8 memory impaired residents in two group homes and hundreds of residents living in the surrounding community.

structed or remodeled) evolve from sound market analysis and are based on careful design and management principles.

2. Facility Design

As the primary long-term care setting for the frail elderly, nursing homes have traditionally been financed and developed under a medical model of care. Current design concepts for long-term care promote a more residential, homelike environment of assisted living wherever possible (Regnier and Pynoos 1987). As a result of continuing changes in design, lenders approach financing with extreme caution. When models change, concerns arise over the potential for functional obsolescence of previously funded projects, with subsequent additional costs of improvement, slow fill-up rates, and vacancies assumed.

Our survey respondents noted that to avoid lender confusion it was urgent to define boundaries for effective, efficient, and desirable operating models. Those designs that follow the more traditional institutional model can expect increasing difficulty in funding and will remain the least popular and most difficult to fill. Facilities whose design follows a more residential and homelike philosophy can be expected to be most accepted and most profitable, especially if prior market analysis has confirmed their need.

3. Facility Management

Since assisted living is a long-term venture for which effective management prototypes are still evolving, investors and lenders who participate in developing projects are often wary. The assisted living philosophy, in focusing on keeping frail and vulnerable elderly out of nursing homes, makes the management component of a project especially important.

Assisted living is a management-intensive enterprise that must satisfy an enormous diversity of needs. Successful management cannot conform to the traditional rigidity of the medically oriented nursing home industry, nor can it be as unstructured as a less professionally managed, family-style, small-scale board-and-care arrangement. In its administrative capacity, management of assisted living transcends roles of planning, organizing, directing, and administering to ensure that the physical, emotional, social, cognitive, and spiritual needs of residents are addressed in a homelike environment. This environment must remain flexible to the changing needs of residents, so that when residents deteriorate to the point of requiring more intensive health care, their needs can be managed.

Assisted living is therefore administratively complex, and the perception of it as a new housing type without clearly defined and effective operating models increases concerns about financial risk.

4. Regulations and Politics

Understanding the peculiarities of policy and regulation surrounding the development of assisted living requires that its development as a component of the residential care industry be viewed within the contexts of housing, long-term care, and finance. These key areas, however, have developed without any integrated perspective or history (Pynoos 1990). Therefore, although the logic of meshing services with housing to provide long-term care is sound, little coherent federal or state policy currently guides these ideas. Furthermore, the incentives to facilitate the process are extremely limited.

Current Policy and Regulations. Effective regulations and their enforcement are crucial, since the people served by assisted living are generally frail, vulnerable, and elderly. State regulations that focus on the assisted living industry are not only limited but very inconsistent, with facilities often regulated by state governments through board-and-care laws. According to reports on the status of associated board-and-care regulation (Hawes, Wildfire, and Lux 1993b; Dobkin 1989), licensing requirements vary greatly from state to state, although federal regulation requires all states to license such facilities. Unfortunately, in some states compliance with inconsistent or contradictory zoning, safety, and health requirements results in a bureaucratic nightmare for those facilities under state and local control.

Oregon was the first state with any semblance of a policy established specifically for assisted living. Since Oregon's legislation became effective in September 1990, Washington, Florida, and New York have developed program standards or regulations that are in demonstration projects or out for bid. New Jersey has a new plan awaiting funding, and North Carolina, Ohio, Massachusetts, and Arizona are currently developing regulations (Mollica et al. 1992). Although many states have yet to make an effort to recognize regulatory needs of the assisted living industry, a national movement is definitely afoot to change the situation. By the year 2000 states without clear regulation should be the exception rather than the rule.

Despite regulatory inconsistencies, federal, state, and local initiatives can be innovative in offering financing incentives for the development, rehabilitation, or upgrading of buildings as assisted living facilities. Varied financing techniques have also been encouraged, making room for acceptance of low-income seniors through rental and service subsidies. Medicaid waivers, historic preservation tax credits, recycled load repayments, housing development subsidies, and creative tax-exempt add-on allowances make up a variety of financing options that differ in implementation nationwide.

Future Regulations. As more consistent regulations do evolve, the potential for increasing costs and extending time frames for development and oc-

FIGURE 5.2. *Design features create intimate scale:* The sloped dormer roof and
the turreted bay window give this room residential scale and character.

cupancy concerns many lenders. The passage of the 1990 OBRA laws, with
funds appropriated by Congress specifically for the assisted living industry,
requires that immediate attention be given to developing appropriate regulations for the assisted living industry. These must be based on design and
management philosophies that support the residential and homelike environment desired, rather than on the traditional regulatory view of aging as
largely a medical problem. Although the new legislation provides limited
funding initially, it has the potential for ultimately making Medicaid funds
available to support the elderly in whatever long-term care option most effectively and cost-efficiently suits their needs.

For the moment, however, apprehension about financing assisted living
is very real, especially if anticipated regulations take on the medically oriented stringency of existing regulations for the nursing home industry.
Many of our respondents suggested that assisted living, even without regulatory barriers, is currently financially safer than standard congregate or
CCRC housing. But in a political arena that has focused on cost containment, deregulation, and promoting transfer of responsibilities to state and
local levels, financial organizations appear hesitant to invest heavily in assisted living.

Nevertheless, a survey of the long-term care industry completed by Laventhol and Horwath (1989) indicates that financing sources are not turning away from housing for the elderly. They are instead "applying prudent standards" to their participation, attempting to ensure that concerns in the four major areas briefly reviewed are addressed.

General Financing Trends

The impact of current political and economic trends on financial institutions can be seen in a quick review of financing trends. Commercial banks continue to dominate the financial scene, most probably reflecting a government-induced shift away from the tax- exempt financing of the early 1980s toward more conventional lending sources.

As a result, an important new kind of housing delivery system has emerged that consists of formally structured partnerships among the corporate, financial, public, and community sectors. Each partner has a specific role in planning, financing, building, and operating housing projects. Variations of these partnerships appear to be very promising financing strategies. These will be reviewed in case studies later in this chapter.

Financial Considerations

Considering the current financial climate and general financing trends, financing of future assisted living housing will be based on careful planning and analysis, with specific strategies in mind. Successful development will also incorporate an understanding of what causes of financial failure. Those causes identified by an AARP report (Dobkin 1989) include the following:

- Overbuilding.
- Overestimation of the value of property, location, or need.
- Overborrowing.
- Depletion of financial reserves.
- Poor marketing to potential residents and inadequate screening of them.
- Financial and operational mismanagement.

Overall, however, the greatest difficulty lies in balancing financing strategies that sometimes appear to conflict. For example, promoting investment objectives that include healthy profits for investors appears to conflict with the larger community need to provide housing for low-income elderly who may not have sufficient funds to cover their residential costs. The case studies in chapter 6 identify facilities that in different ways have developed financing strategies through attention to a series of financial principles.

These principles recognize that attention to financing is the key to the successful implementation of any assisted living project. They therefore attempt to identify the range of considerations that can be used to judge the financing strategy selected. Derived from existing literature and integrated with attitudes toward financing expressed by assisted living sponsors contacted during the course of our study, the ten principles are the following:

1. *Encourage reduction of project costs without impacting quality.* Effective financing keeps costs as low as possible while maintaining attention to a quality product that meets consumer desires.

2. *Balance leverage versus equity contribution.* Structure financing so that levels of debt and/or equity contribution consider both current economic uncertainties and high development costs.

3. *Spread investment risk.* Limit risk by spreading investments over time and parties involved, such as taking advantage of deferred payments or utilizing joint-venture partners.

4. *Promote both investment and social objectives.* Effective financial agendas consider the value in meeting "social" objectives as a sound strategy toward achieving the friendly, homelike, quality environment that ensures maximum occupancy and secures investments.

5. *Enhance economic feasibility.* Financial viability of any assisted living facility involves ensuring economic success through sound strategies implemented during initial phases of development, construction, and ongoing operation; target market assessment; and premarketing.

6. *Preserve affordability.* Ensure that access to assisted living remains open to frail elderly of differing financial means by increasing affordability through use of subsidies and maintaining a balance between self-paying and subsidized residents.

7. *Reduce long-term investment risk potential.* Pay attention to each step of the financing process, beginning with an accurate target market assessment and continuing with regular evaluations of both current and potential short-term and long-term strategies.

8. *Prioritize cash/earnings while maximizing cash flow security.* Set

FIGURE 5.3. *Single loaded balcony corridor is shaped to accommodate a place to sit:* A small table and two chairs adjacent to the unit entry door overlook an enclosed atrium garden below.

resident rates at appropriate levels to ensure adequate profits while maximizing cash flow security through consistent occupancy rates.

9. *Balance low-income/self-paying resident mix.* Take advantage of both public and private funding options by employing effective management strategies to attract a balance of self-paying and low-income subsidized residents.

10. *Expand resource options by encouraging partnerships.* Through coordination of both public and private resources, expand options available for financing, designing, developing, managing, operating, and effectively promoting the assisted living philosophy.

Strategic Financial Principles

A comprehensive model of assisted living should consider the ten principles just reviewed and their implications not only to financing but to the design and management of facilities. Successful facilities incorporate financing strategies as the vehicle for implementing design concepts and management philosophies. The following section describes the preceding principles in more detail.

1. Encourage Reduction of Project Costs Without Impacting Quality

In times of economic uncertainty the government emphasis on cost containment affects the public sector, whereas the private sector focuses on limiting unnecessary spending that affects profitability. Financing strategies that seem most effective consider these trends and operate to encourage the development of quality facilities while minimizing the costs of development and subsequent operation.

Costs for assisted living facilities reflect physical design, the service package, and the clientele serviced. Start-up costs are often high as a result of ensuring that a personal-care service package is available as soon as the facility is ready for occupancy. When this is combined with a long rent-up period, the availability of working capital becomes especially important, since initial operating deficits may be high.

A realistic occupancy level is very important if operating costs are to be reduced. For some assisted living facilities it is not unusual for this level to approach 100 percent to break even. To hedge against the risk involved, innovative financing strategies attempt to retain a lower than normal loan-to-value ratio by obtaining multiple sources of funding to supplement the mortgage.

Effective Design Strategies. Controls must be incorporated to ensure that project costs are managed from the outset rather than through a last-ditch effort to balance the budget. Reducing costs by downgrading the decorative elements of carpeting, wall trimmings, and landscaping, for example, affects the quality of the facility negatively and may therefore backfire as a cost-saving measure. As Paul Klaassen of Sunrise Retirement Homes notes, daily costs of these niceties for an average-sized unit amount to no more than fifty cents when amortized over thirty years. Moreover, the increased pleasure they provide residents in making their environment homelike make such costs immediately recoupable.

Value engineering has been effective because it ensures that every design decision has an associated value. Decisions to reduce costs can be made at the beginning and throughout the course of the project rather than at the end to balance the budget.

A further plan to reduce costs is through design-and-build strategies that promote negotiation between general contractors and designers. These match the strengths and capabilities of both contractors and designers in meeting the needs of the facility being developed. By adjusting the design before finalizing it, contracts that might otherwise have been padded to minimize contractor risk can be negotiated at reduced cost.

Where projects provide affordable housing for low-income residents, tax-exempt bond financing, low-income tax credits, and public/private

FIGURE 5.4. *French doors increase daylight and access:* Double French doors are used between the bedroom and the living room in a typical Rosewood Estate dwelling unit.

partnerships can be utilized. In addition, fast-track permit processing can allow for cost reductions without diminishing quality.

2. Balance Leverage Versus Equity Contribution

Past housing projects have generally been highly leveraged, maximizing debt rather than equity financing. Their high loan-to-value ratios enabled developers to retain greater shares of equity and ultimate residual values at the time of sale or refinancing. In addition, debt financing was more prevalent because equity investors, who take greater risks, anticipate a much higher return than lenders over the term of the investment. Prior to the Tax Reform Act of 1986, financing using tax-exempt bonds of varying kinds was much more prevalent.

The Browning Residence in Vermont used this form of financing in its private placement of a small-issue tax-exempt industrial development bond that raised approximately 57 percent of the total development funds. The Tax Reform Act of 1986 eliminated such an option (Council of State Housing Agencies and National Association of State Units on Aging 1987). In reducing traditional tax benefits that accompanied ownership through decreasing the availability of tax-exempt bond financing, it refocused thinking on increasing the equity component of financing housing construction.

In the assisted living industry the risk of foreclosure because of operating difficulties is much less in projects financed with minimal loans. In new construction projects with high debt levels it may take up to three years before the facility becomes operationally stable. Although it remains possible to finance projects through 100 percent equity financing, a balance between debt and equity seems far more practical, given current economic concerns about high development costs.

Minimizing equity contribution can include manipulation of payment schedules through creative amortization, partial amortization, or graduated mortgage payments, but financing appears most feasible at a level of 60 to 70 percent debt. Creation of an equity fund based on the syndication of tax credits has proved an efficient way of obtaining equity money for housing projects in general.

3. Spread Investment Risk

Average estimated costs of building construction or major adaptive renovations to develop an assisted living facility range from seventy to one hundred dollars per square foot. Adding a 40–50 percent factor for corridors and common spaces, a medium-sized one-bedroom unit of 450 square feet could range between $80,000 and $100,000, with land an additional cost per unit. Even in a smaller facility of twelve to fifteen units this represents a substantial investment. Moreover, costs can vary markedly, depending on the geographic location (e.g., urban versus rural, midwestern versus southwestern states), the facility size, or the strategy employed in developing a purpose-built facility or one adapted for reuse.

Financing strategies that incorporate multiple investment sources and varying options for long- and short-term payback and that involve long-term participation of residents in assuming risk limit potential risk by spreading investments over time and parties involved. Such strategies often include syndications or contracts between developers and equity capital investors, joint ventures, or public and private partnerships.

4. Promote Both Investment and Social Objectives

Effective financial strategies that operate from a perspective of enlightened self-interest consider the meeting of social objectives a sound business strategy. Achieving the friendly, homelike, quality environment that ensures maximum occupancy and secures investments requires a supportive management philosophy focused on innovation and flexibility. This keeps residents well and out of institutions for as long as possible. With this in mind, ensuring long-term financial security requires maintaining a balance between investment return for owners and the assurance that residents have adequate personal care even while their finances dwindle. Consequently, creative financial arrangements may be necessary if the target market includes residents unable to meet their lease obligations fully with their own resources.

Historically, the social objective of providing appropriate housing has been met by the public sector, but recent financing strategies encourage the private sector to become more active in this area while meeting their investment objectives. Promoting such objectives often includes maximizing short-term cash flow or tax incentives, long-term residual benefits, tax shelters with growth potential, and endowment or charitable contributions as well as maintaining an effective resident assessment program prior to and during residence.

5. Enhance Economic Feasibility

The short- and long-term financial viability of an assisted living facility depends on successfully negotiating the phases of unoccupied development and occupied operation. Proper planning, design, and management prior to and during development can speed development and limit carrying costs. Moreover, a competitive advantage can result from ensuring that the building does not take on the institutional look of a nursing home.

Once development is assured, marketing efforts must continually target potential residents and their families. As a strategy for enhancing economic feasibility, marketing constantly aims at getting potential residents and the community at large involved in the assisted living project. Not only must the facility be strongly marketed, but so must the philosophy of assisted living, which promotes the well-being of frail elderly in a noninstitutional environment. The ability to maintain high occupancy rates will be only as good as the original market assessment that confirmed the need.

Once a project is developed, its economic feasibility can be enhanced by using state and local initiatives, fund raising, and refinancing arrangements. Reducing costs, however, should never impinge on the ideal of providing quality care. Therefore it is extremely important to recognize that features added to increase the homelike quality of the assisted living environment ultimately can increase the economic feasibility of the project. Such features should more than pay for themselves.

The financial viability of a project can often be enhanced by using creative supplemental methods. For assisted living these might include local economic assistance grants, density bonuses, or land enhancements that encourage landowners to contribute land as equity or carryback loans.

6. Preserve Affordability

Financing assisted living can be problematic if there are fewer middle-income residents who can afford the fees than there are lower-income residents who cannot. Evaluating long-term affordability needs is a primary element of preliminary financial planning. Residency must be affordable; therefore innovations in establishing sliding-fee scales for varying components of personal care are important. Subsidies can also help preserve affordability through the use of state or local initiatives (e.g., Medicaid 2176) or through agencies that provide services billed at minimal rates.

In general, strategies that maximize the number of immediately affordable units for the target market seem more effective than those that focus on long-term affordability. This is particularly true where communities include large groups of low-income elderly whose only housing alternative is an inappropriate institution.

In some facilities design strategies have been employed for indigent residents that allow single-room occupancy units that maintain levels of privacy but share bathroom and kitchen facilities.

7. Reduce Long-Term Investment Risk Potential

Reducing long-term investment risk is a process that begins prior to any assisted living facility development, through adequate attention to each step of the financing process. Investment strategies that appear the most effective balance the potential investment risk in both the short term and long term. Among these are accelerating payments, eliminating contingencies, or limiting liability.

8. Prioritize Cash/Earnings While Maximizing Cash Flow Security

Extended lease-up periods as a normal part of the development of a project can result in heavy drains on cash flow. But later lease-up periods can be protracted, and unnecessary costs can result if rental charges are too high. Although it is important to set resident fees appropriately to ensure adequate profit and anticipate reasonable changes in operating costs, it is also important to maximize cash flow by ensuring high occupancy rates.

Prioritizing cash/earnings while maximizing cash flow security can be accomplished in many ways, including such investment vehicles as Real Estate Mortgage Investment Conduits (REMICS) or Master Limited Partnerships, which offer investment diversity.

9. Balance the Mix of Subsidized Low Income and Self-Paying Middle Income Residents

Flexible strategies enable facilities to take advantage of both public and private financing. However, the resident mix must combine low-income government-supported seniors with self-paying residents. To satisfy community housing goals, this means that as many as 30 percent of residents may need to be low to moderate income. This can result in management strategies that become intertwined with financing approaches. To avoid policy conflicts between residents of differing financial status low-income and self-paying residents must be balanced. To reduce costs while increasing the number of low-income residents, sponsors have promoted small units initially designed to share bathroom and shower facilities rather than arriving at double occupancy as an afterthought to reduce costs. (See the Frederick case study in chapter 6.)

Figure 5.5. *Institutional counters with wire glass partitions are unnecessary:* A wood, free standing desk in the entry of this Wisconsin nursing center appears friendly and approachable.

10. Expand Resource Options by Encouraging Partnerships

We shall use the term *public/private partnerships* to refer to ongoing collaborative ventures involving both public- and private-sector participants whose goal is the successful implementation of assisted living facilities. Partnerships can be project based, involving corporate sponsors that work directly with community groups or with state or local governments. Such ventures focus on the completion of a single assisted living facility and are therefore customized to the individual circumstances of the project.

Alternatively, assisted living facilities are being developed through more formal, permanent, program-based partnerships that combine resources for many projects, thereby producing financing efficiencies.

Partnership arrangements for developing assisted living facilities bring an array of resources together to focus collectively on goals. Participants generally belong to either the public sector or the private sector. As can be seen in chapter 6, arrangements among these groups can vary considerably, in response to local needs. Public/private partnerships fit in well with many of the preceding financing strategies. They allow varying resources to be combined and coordinated toward the goal of producing affordable housing, including that within the assisted living industry.

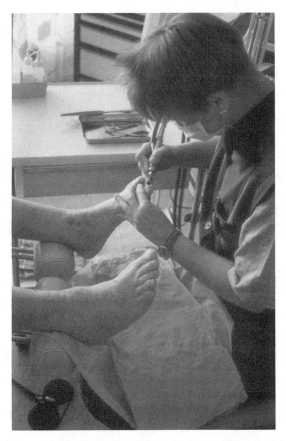

FIGURE 5.6. *Access to a range of services and diagnostic analysis is important:* Podiatry is a necessary service for many older people with circulatory problems or diabetes.

A comprehensive model of assisted living should consider these ten principles and their impact not only in establishing an effective financing strategy, but in supporting principles of design and management presented in previous chapters. For example, enhancing the economic feasibility of a project in which many low-income residents will live may mean building single-room occupancy units that share facilities. As noted in the design chapter, environmental design and organizational management policies must be coordinated with this financing strategy to ensure that each individual's privacy is maintained and the environment is made suitable for sharing. The response to the financing principle of enhancing economic feasibility, like that to most of the other principles, therefore impacts the physical environment, the facility's policies, and the management philosophies of the staff.

Categories of Financial Diversity

Financial diversity as it relates to senior housing involves considerably more tools than have historically been available to other forms of housing. Historically, nonprofit organizations, especially religious groups, financed development of continuing-care retirement communities (CCRCs) through nonrefundable endowments, church funds, and different types of bonds. During the 1970s and early 1980s the U.S. Department of Housing and Urban Development (HUD) became a major financial backer of these programs. However, recent changes in the housing finance system have developed a more flexible system than the one that existed in the 1970s (Tuccillo and Goodman 1983). The Reagan administration's program in housing finance was aimed at three goals:

1. Reducing the effect of the federal government on the economy.
2. Increasing the involvement of the private sector in business and industry.
3. Fostering new mortgage instruments to provide an adequate and affordable flow of funds to industry.

As a result, regulatory reform during the Reagan era viewed housing as a commodity rather than an important national objective. Consequently, as government financing has become less available (especially as a result of the severely restricting effect of the 1986 Tax Reform Act) and as privatization has been increasingly emphasized, many private-sector developers have become involved in senior housing, including assisted living. Unfortunately, with few subsidized units available, this has resulted in an overbuilding of the middle-class market. However, developers like Sunrise Retirement Homes have made a corporate commitment to serve low-income elderly residents. They devote approximately 10 percent of their units to low-income residents, who are effectively subsidized by private-pay residents. If this attitude was adopted by all private developers, a major step toward obtaining assisted living units for the low-income frail elderly could be taken.

Financing Tools Available Today

Both public- and private-sector financial techniques are employed to finance development and the ongoing operation of assisted living facilities. Development costs include the purchase of land, design and legal fees (soft costs), site development, and construction (Mollica et al. 1992). Financing mechanisms also exist to cover the debt service on construction loans and to supplement fees for resident care. Moreover, supplementary strategies can be employed to adhere more easily to the previously cited financing principles. Although they are not exhaustive of all strategies available, techniques that appear to best represent the financing options available for assisted living include many of those presented by the National Association of Homebuilders in their handbook (NAHB 1987) and updated by a recent publication from the Center for Vulnerable Populations (Mollica et al. 1992). The private sector has in number financed most assisted living for the frail elderly, although the number of public programs has increased recently.

Public Sector Financing

Tax-Exempt Bonds

Bonds are securities that constitute a contract in which a borrower (assisted living developer) agrees to repay lenders (state, local, or federal government) in full at some future date and to pay interest on specified dates from the date of borrowing until the date of repayment. Tax-exempt bonds have financed a great deal of the existing senior housing and were a popular way to reduce project costs. However, the Tax Reform Act of 1986 brought major changes in tax-exempt financing criteria. States are now limited to annual volume caps for private-purpose tax-exempt bond issues of $50 per capita or $150 million, whichever is greater.

In addition, eligibility requirements for rental projects financed by tax-exempt bonds were tightened, so that 20 percent of all units must be reserved for tenants earning up to 50 percent of the median income for the area, or 40 percent of all units must be reserved for tenants earning up to 60 percent of the median income for the area. In conjunction with a low-income rental housing tax credit of 4 percent annually for ten years, tax-exempt bonds remain useful for reducing project fund costs and balancing investment and social objectives, but they are no longer as popular as they were before the 1986 tax reform (CSHA and NASUA 1987).

Taxable Bonds

Financing from taxable bonds is similar to that from tax-exempt bonds, except that the federal regulations for reservation of low-income units do not apply and yields are somewhat higher.

HUD Section 202 Improvements

Under Section 202, formerly known as Housing for the Elderly and Handicapped, HUD subsidizes low-income seniors' rental housing through a limited amount of funding. Historically, this has been a direct forty-year loan from HUD to a nonprofit sponsoring organization at a low interest rate. Each year HUD publishes a notification of fund availability that confirms the amount of funding and units available for the area. Sponsors then bid competitively for the funds, unless the total mortgage amount is less than $2 million or the market rents do not exceed HUD's published fair market rents for the area by 110 percent.

The HUD 202 program replaces the combination of mortgage loans and Section 8 rental subsidies with capital advances that cover construction, rehabilitation and some acquisition costs, and project rental assistance. The cash advances are actually grants that do not need to be repaid if the development meets targets for very-low-income occupancy rates for forty years.

Most of the prior discussion of assisted living design, management, and financing assumes that assisted living refers to a purpose-built housing arrangement. With the passage of the 1990 Affordable Housing Act, Congress appropriated funds for the identification of HUD service coordinators to provide or coordinate delivery of a package of services in support of an assisted living environment that follows a service overlay model.

Section 232 Mortgage Insurance

Although Section 232 mortgage insurance, which is a HUD/FHA program, was originally designed for nursing homes and intermediate-care facilities, an expansion in 1985 included board-and-care homes (Mollica et al. 1992). Definition of eligibility qualifies many assisted living facilities—"a type of residential facility that provides room, board, and continuous protective oversight" for "individuals who cannot live independently but who do not require the more extensive care offered by intermediate-care facilities or nursing homes." New construction or substantial rehabilitation can both be covered by the mortgage to be insured, although public entities such as local housing authorities are ineligible.

Although Section 232 does not provide for rental assistance or subsidize ongoing operational costs, it can assist developers in obtaining long-term mortgage loans to cover construction. HUD offices provide the insurance after the developer or owner locates mortgage financing through a lender approved by FHA. Mortgages insured under the 232 program have a maximum forty-year term and a 90 percent loan-to-value ratio.

Residential units in an eligible facility can include shared bedrooms and baths for up to four people or individual efficiency or single-bedroom apartments. Other requirements include central dining, kitchen, lounge, and recreation areas; continuous protective oversight; and three meals a day. However, program guidelines can limit assisted living facilities severely, since the calculations of cost per unit force developers to design double-occupancy rooms without kitchens unless they can find alternative financing to meet the extra cost of single-occupancy units with kitchens and bathrooms. In addition, although low- and moderate-income residents need not be the targeted resident base, a 10 percent equity requirement makes it difficult for nonprofit organizations to comply with guidelines.

Congregate Housing Services Program

The HUD Congregate Housing Services Program (CHSP) provides eligible states and local government and nonprofit agencies with five-year grants for service coordination and supportive services in Sections 202, 236, 221(d), and 8 and public housing projects. Services can then be provided under contract with external agencies.

In its provision of services CHSP simulates many standard components of assisted living, although because it is a HUD program, concerns over delivering medical care in HUD-sponsored facilities restrict delivery of nursing care using project funds.

Conceptually, CHSP offers a financing mechanism for facilitating aging in place in HUD buildings. Regulations, a program handbook, and funding levels were expected to allow funding in late 1993. However, with only 100 projects nationwide, an average of about two per state, CHSP certainly will not make major headway in delivering assisted living services to low-income frail elderly.

Tax Credits: Historical Preservation and Low-Income Housing

Public and private housing joint ventures focus increasingly on ways to adapt vacant or obsolete structures to economically viable and productive uses. Current provisions of the Internal Revenue Code substantially influence preservation and reuse of historic properties and specifically encourage investment in their rehabilitation rather than in new construction. With several provisions, renovation of a historic building may qualify for a historic preservation tax credit equal to 25 percent of the cost of rehabilitation. Related to the restoration of a historic building for the purpose of becoming an assisted living project, the property must be a "certified historic structure" as determined by the secretary of the interior, who must also confirm that the reconstruction work is consistent with the historic character of the property or district. Rehabilitation must cost more than $5,000 or the adjusted basis of the building (whichever is greater), and at least 75 percent of the existing external walls must remain in place as external walls.

Investment in low-income housing was given a boost through a new low-income housing tax incentive program created by the 1986 Tax Reform Act. It allows developers or owners of housing with some low-income residents to receive credit against their tax liability over a ten-year period (Mollica et al. 1992). Investors buy credits to raise cash for a project, which then reduces the subsequent amount of debt financing required. These credits are calculated as a percentage of the funds spent on construction, rehabilitation, or acquisition for the low-income-resident portion of the housing development. (In 1991 the average tax credit allocation was $4,000 per unit, with investors paying approximately forty-five cents for each dollar of credit.)

Volumes of tax credits are controlled in two ways: either under an annual state volume cap or for projects financed through tax-exempt bonds, which are themselves subject to state volume caps.

As with tax-exempt bonds, 20 percent of the units must be for residents at or below 50 percent of the area median income, or 40 percent of the units must be for residents at or below 60 percent of the area median income. Rents are capped at 30 percent of the income level that qualifies a resident for the facility. Although program incentives encourage even longer time frames, these restrictions are actually locked in for a minimum of fifteen years.

Since states can make assisted living a priority for use of their tax credits, this financing mechanism could provide a valuable tool for targeting services to the frail elderly whose income is low. However, it is a complex process, and varying IRS interpretations and state policies can make use of tax credits in assisted living facilities particularly awkward.

Medicaid Waivers

Federal Medicaid matching funds allow states to provide for nonmedical services under the Section 2176 waiver authority. Through this waiver, low-income individuals at risk of institutionalization can receive community-based services that are not covered under the state Medicaid plan. Frail elderly who are eligible for nursing home care and who reside in an assisted living program *that does not have rent subsidies* qualify for Medicaid waivers (Mollica et al. 1992).

States can use their Medicaid waivers to serve predetermined numbers of frail elderly, thereby limiting their fiscal liability. In addition, they must meet a cost effectiveness test. The Department of Health and Human Services (DHHS) requires that states show that the cost to Medicaid of providing services to individuals under the waiver is not more than that of providing services without the waiver. Along with their flexible service package, states can set higher-income eligibility levels to accommodate people living in the community who would otherwise be ineligible for Medicaid.

Few states have attempted to use this subsidy for residents of assisted living facilities as yet, although the experience in Oregon suggests that we can expect to see a growing interest in this area. Medicaid waivers deal with a major gap caused by the absence of rent subsidies and financing for the low-income frail elderly population.

Private Sector Financing

Savings and Loans

Conventional loans remain available for the development of assisted living facilities that provide housing for self-paying residents (mostly middle- or upper-income elderly). Loans vary, from simple land development loans to complex participating mortgages. However, deals are negotiated directly with the savings and loan officers, and as a result of the infancy of the assisted living industry, they have not always been easy to obtain. Available loan structures include the following:

- Adjustable-rate loans tied to an index, such as the Cost of Funds Index.
- Negative amortization loans that take advantage of repayment

schedules synchronized with increases in net operating income that occur as occupancy rates stabilize.

- Participating mortgages that increase the economic feasibility of a project by reducing long-term investment risks by exchanging low permanent loan rates for a percentage of the cash flow and residual cash proceeds at the time the property is eventually sold.

Commercial Banks

As with most retirement community development, commercial banks have been the primary source of financing for assisted living development. Construction loans tied to the permanent loan take-out amount are available on a prime-plus basis. However, commercial banks look for developers with experience, a successful track record, and financial strength. Often this encourages the development of a partnership or joint venture between parties who each offer differing skills in the development of the financial package. For developing facilities primarily for low-income residents, commercial banks offer little without substantial equity to reduce loan levels.

Traditional loans have been considered the easiest and cheapest to obtain for most private middle- and upper-income resident-based facilities. However, as investors, especially wealthy foreign sponsors, continue to demand condensed investment time frames and faster return on investment, short-term (five- to seven-year) floating-rate loans have become more popular. Such changes in investment philosophy encourage a trend toward quick-turnaround building acquisition and renovation rather than original time-consuming construction with long-term investment potential.

Insurance Companies

Insurance companies could be a major source of funding for assisted living, since pension funds represent the largest and fastest-growing pool of funds for housing projects. Unlike savings and loan agreements, however, financing with insurance companies must be arranged through an investment banker or mortgage broker. Typically, these deals are available only for larger-facility developers or for assisted living as a component of a large continuing-care retirement community.

Life insurance companies are limited to specific kinds of investments by the state laws under which they are chartered. These laws typically define the percentage of assets that can be invested in particular types of investments and the maximum loan-to-value ratio for mortgage investments.

Real Estate Investment Trusts

Real Estate Investment Trusts (REITs) typically involve corporations, associations, or trusts organized for the purpose of pooling real estate investment funds. They have generally been popular in the sale and leaseback of nursing homes in which the REIT purchases a property from an operator for 90 to 100 percent of its appraised value and then leases it back to the operator. For facility operators this form of financing is attractive, since it makes equity available for renovations, working capital, or future developments. The option to purchase the facility at fair market value during the lease term is also often specified. Although REITs offer flexibility in structuring financial arrangements to meet a company's objectives, they are highly restricted by a myriad of tax and state securities regulations.

Investment Funds

Depending on investment objectives and the level of credit, a variety of investment funds, both taxable and tax-exempt, are available. Most are structured as partnerships that allow benefits to flow to investors without double taxation, because many investors are tax-exempt. For example, many make taxable investments in tax-deferred accounts, such as individual retirement accounts (IRAs) or Keoghs.

Many of the funds invest in participating first mortgage loans, which is an attractive form of financing that offers below-market interest rates in exchange for participation in future economic benefits. However, such a tie to long-term performance necessitates close scrutiny and selectivity of deals financed.

Syndications

Syndications involve selling limited-partnership interests in income-producing properties. The risks and rewards of ownership are shared, so that investors join with a developer or syndicate, making the project feasible and providing needed equity. A partnership is the finance mechanism used to syndicate the equity or ownership interest, so that investors need not be involved in the actual management of the project. The main interest in such an arrangement is to share the economic benefits of tax losses, cash flow, and appreciation. This means that limited partners in a syndication are generally interested in their eligibility for tax credits, depreciation, or deduction of a large proportion of their investment as soon as possible in their

FIGURE 5.7. *Mixed use housing is less common in the United States:* This Swedish project mixes family housing on the upper floor with a 6 unit home for demented frail older people on the first floor.

ownership term; in their ability to deduct other costs during project development; and in tax code restrictions or penalties assessed at the resale of the project. Low-income rehabilitated housing can elect a 200 percent declining-balance method of calculating depreciation (rather than 175 percent) and can depreciate over fifteen years rather than the traditional eighteen-year period.

For nonprofit sponsors, however, investors' financial goals and socially motivated priorities may conflict. Nevertheless the benefits include the following:

- The availability of a new source of capital.
- The ability to take advantage of tax subsidies normally of no use to nonprofit sponsors.
- The availability of sophisticated expertise in financing tax-sensitive investments, meeting securities laws, and managing property.

In addition, the nonprofit sponsor must be tax-exempt, so that interest on any sinking fund established to acquire property would not be taxable. Nor-

mally, however, the sinking fund would not generate enough funds for this
to be a major problem.

Real Estate Mortgage Investment Conduits

Real estate mortgage investment conduits (REMICs) are formed to hold
mortgages secured by interests in real property, in the name of a corporation, partnership, or trust. Because REMIC security sales can be treated as
asset sales rather than as debts for accounting purposes, they offer a high
degree of accounting flexibility.

Supplementary Financing Strategies

Land Enhancements

Since land is actually a major portion of the expense in financing a project,
overall project costs or equity requirements can be reduced significantly by
obtaining land creatively. To make projects viable, landowners may become
limited partners by contributing the land; they may contribute it at a highly

FIGURE 5.8. *Adjustable awnings control sunlight and add color:* Electric controls in each unit allow these shading devices to be easily manipulated.

reduced rate in order to retain control; or they may carry the land as a second mortgage for several years at a below-market interest rate.

Zoning Changes

Zoning codes often restrict the building density (i.e., the number of units allowed on a site). However, costs per unit can be reduced substantially by obtaining a density variance that changes the zoning code to allow an increase in the density of units per acre. In this way project feasibility is significantly enhanced.

Deferred Loans

Use of deferred loans as project subsidies is the most cost-effective means of leveraging private dollars for rehabilitation, since repayment of any principal and interest due is postponed until sale or refinancing of a property. Since no monthly payment is required with a deferred loan, all the net cash flow available for debt service from an assisted living rental project can be used to underwrite private borrowing. This creates maximum leverage.

Joint Ventures

Today, with an increasing need for innovation in financial arrangements in order to implement housing projects for seniors, joint ventures and limited partnerships that involve both the public and private sectors are becoming increasingly familiar. They satisfy the need to meet equity requirements while spreading the risk among multiple investors. Moreover, a joint venture expands the opportunity for a builder or developer to increase both construction and management volume. Finally, joint ventures with sound financial institutions provide invaluable opportunities to develop long-term relationships with an ongoing funding source.

6. Seven Case Studies

Seven projects have been selected to demonstrate the "best practice" approaches from the preceding chapters. Figure 6.1 locates facilities throughout the United States. Facilities have been selected that provide unique financial and management strategies. They also represent projects with differences resulting from varying target populations, facility size, and profit or nonprofit sponsorship. However, each facility includes some aspect of financing directed toward moderate- to low-income elderly.

FIGURE 6.1. *Site Locations of Seven Case Studies*

TABLE 6.1

Financial Principles Primary to Each Assisted Living Facility

FINANCING PRINCIPLES	Rackleff House	Paddock Kensington	Eaton Terrace II	Woodside Place	Rosewood Estate	Linconia Center	Sunrise of Frederick
1. Reduce project costs without affecting quality	X	X	X	X	X	X	X
2. Balance leverage vs. equity		X	X	X			X
3. Spread investment risk			X	X		X	
4. Promote investment and social objectives	X	X	X	X	X		X
5. Enhance economic feasibility	X			X			X
6. Preserve affordability	X	X	X	X	X	X	X
7. Reduce long-term investment risk	X		X	X			X
8. Prioritize cash/earnings, maximize cash flow		X		X	X		X
9. Balance low-income/self-pay resident mix	X	X	X	X			
10. Expand resource options through partnerships		X	X	X		X	X

Although many other facilities have noteworthy features, these represent a broad spectrum of development options and choices. Many characterize promising current and future trends. Table 6.1 presents these facilities in a matrix that connects each to the financing principles presented in the previous chapter. Although each facility has to some degree addressed each financing principle, those presented in the table represent primary financing goals.

In an effort to provide benchmarks for comparing these case study exemplars, Table 6.2 has been constructed with a variety of pertinent demographic and project-related characteristics. Where available, statistics have been included that present facts regarding the resident population and the building, enabling interfacility comparisons.

Rackleff House: Canby, Oregon

Facility Overview

Rackleff House, in Canby, Oregon, is an example of a small facility, creatively developed as one of a number of successful assisted living demon-

FIGURE **6.2.** *Rackleff House, Canby Oregon*

stration projects established in Oregon in the late 1980s. A single-story licensed facility opened in mid-1990, it contains twenty-five residential units
and serves a rural community in a self-contained assisted living setting.

Innovations in Financing and Management

Developmental Strategy. Rackleff House emphasizes the most innovative
features of Oregon's assisted living model and serves a substantial low-
income elderly population. It was developed initially through state housing
bonds and is operationally subsidized through the Medicaid 1915 program
that pays for the personal-care services of approximately 40 to 50 percent of
its residents. Philosophies of management and design have been incorporated with financing mechanisms to provide quality service to frail vulnerable elderly, regardless of income. The focus of investors remains on prioritizing long-term resale potential rather than on maximizing short-term
cash flow. However, operational costs are maintained close to a break-even
level.

Through its initial development and construction stage, Rackleff House
was privately financed by a conventional loan through First Interstate Bank.
Long-term financing was then obtained by buying down the original loan

TABLE 6.2
General Characteristics of Case Study Facilities

Characteristics	Rackleff house	Paddock Kensington	Eaton Terrace II	Woodside Place	Rosewood Estate	Lincolnia Center	Sunrise of Frederick
State Located	Oregon	Nebraska	Colorado	Pennsylvania	Minnesota	Virginia	Maryland
Number of units	25	65	65	30	68	26	60
Context: suburban, small town	Small town	Small town	Suburban	Suburban	Suburban	Suburban	Small town
Type of facility	Assisted living	Assisted living	Assisted living	Alzheimer's care	Assisted living	Assisted living	Assisted living
Number of building levels	1	5	6	1	3	3(2nd floor A/L)	3 + BSMT
Site size—(in acres)	1.3	2.0	1.0	3.0	1.9	5.25	1.0
Cost of Project	$975,000	$2,700,000	$4,172,000	$2,600,000	$5,000,000	$8,000,000*	$6,000,000
Financing approach	Conventional using state bonds	Private syndicate	Public/private partnership	Public/private partnership	HUD 221 (d) 4	Public partnership	Conventional with equity partner
Gross building area (sq. ft.)	15,800	47,900	47,400	23,000	62,700	61,400*	48,200

Daily cost of service	$33–$55/day	$25–$36/day	$40–$48/day	$20–$86/day	$65–$80/day	*Not calculable	$25–$110/day
Single/double occupancy Studio/1-bedroom (BDR)	21 studio 4 1 BDR	31 studio 34 1 & 2 BDR	56 SO 9 DO	24 SO 6 DO	20 studio 48 1 BDR	0 SO 26 DO	39 studio 21 1 BDR
Average unit size (sq. ft.)	315	300	345	180	500	386	340
Average age of residents	85	86	85	80.8	82.5	84	82
Number of residents	24	43	72	36	69	52	88
Number of couples	1–2	3	0	0	4	1	4
% Residents needing bathing assistance	89%	40%	53%	92%	50%	85%	40%
% Confused residents	60%	2%	25%	100%	20%	50%	50%
% Incontinent residents	40%	20%	20%	28%	6%	21%	20%
% Residents needing toileting assistance	52%	0%	0%	59%	30%	15%	20%
% Ambulatory residents**	80%	100%	100%	100%	53%	100%	90%

* Facility includes senior center, independent housing and assisted living.
** Residents confined to wheelchairs not included in ambulatory counts

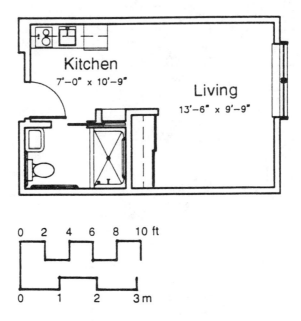

FIGURE 6.3. *Studio unit:* Although small in size, this plan has adequate space in the bathroom and offers a small kitchen for food preparation.

using Oregon State housing bonds, issued with the restriction that 40 percent of the facility be made available for Medicaid residents. The target population therefore became low- and middle-income elderly rather than the traditional higher-income residents generally served by assisted living facilities. With a philosophy based on community commitment, Rackleff House focused a modest marketing campaign on ensuring that it became an unmistakable feature of Canby, recognized as permanently addressing specific community needs.

The integration of financial and marketing strategies focused on ensuring quality of care for those who needed it. One hundred percent occupancy was reached within the first three months of operation. Although this can be viewed as a function of limited local competition and high need, it also confirms the value of a sound market assessment prior to embarking on such a project. As a result, the economic feasibility of the facility was enhanced and ensured even prior to completion of the building.

Medicaid Waivers for Low-Income Elderly. Within the framework of our study Rackleff House's financing process is particularly noteworthy as an example of maintaining ongoing operations and preserving the affordability of rental units for low-income elderly. Residents are screened by state-appointed Medicaid case managers who maintain a high degree of flexibility in determining the eligibility of low-income residents for admission to nursing homes. Those who are eligible can choose to obtain nonmedical services in assisted living (or other community-based) facilities, receiving Medicaid funds for payment of these services under the Section 1915 waiver authority. Reimbursement rates vary according to the level of service deemed necessary by the Medicaid case manager, as developed through state negotiations with providers of service types. Level of service varies according to extent of impairment. For assisted living facilities the rates continue to be reasonably favorable, adequate, and fair, although this is not true for similar community-based housing alternatives.

At Rackleff House a relatively similar differentiation of service levels exists, so that those requiring the most intensive services pay the highest rate and are reimbursed accordingly. For recipients of Medicaid subsidies the difference between rental costs and the corresponding Medicaid reimbursement rate declines with increased service level, as depicted in Table 6.2. From a management perspective, reimbursement comes very close to meeting actual operating costs.

Medicaid rules allow double occupancy to reduce individual costs and to increase the facility income derived from the waiver program. However, since the management philosophy of Rackleff House focuses on independence with privacy, this practice is discouraged unless the couple is married or has a long-term friendship. To date only one unit is double occupied, by a married couple.

TABLE 6.3

Rackleff House Monthly Costs by Service Level for Private Pay and Medicaid Residents

Rackleff house monthly costs (studio unit)		Medicaid reimbursement rates for assisted living		
Service level	Cost	Service level	Cost	Differential
I	$1,249	II	$974	22.01%
II	$1,449	III	$1,182	18.42%
III	$1,649	IV	$1,442	12.55%

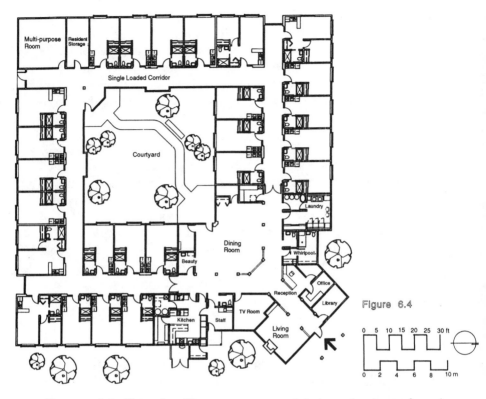

FIGURE 6.4. *Floor plan:* The compact courtyard design makes it easy for residents to access common spaces. Note the single loaded corridor that introduces natural light and an attractive view of the courtyard from the rear.

Lessons Learned with Potential for External Application

Impact of Size on Facility Success. Success at Rackleff House has depended not only on the creativity of its financing process, but also on the innovations associated with its design and management approach. With a capacity of only twenty-five units and a square-courtyard-shaped footprint, Rackleff House's layout encourages movement. The small size of the facility has encouraged independence even more than originally anticipated, and residents can access public spaces with minimal assistance. As a result, their functional level improves. In many cases residents have been discharged to lower levels of service as they improved.

Management by Vertical Integration. In such a small facility difficulties with staffing depth and the need for any staff member to respond to any resident need were expected to cause major personnel problems. The encouragement of vertical service integration has resolved most anticipated staffing problems, to the benefit of residents and the improvement of staff performance. Staff members have been trained in a variety of tasks and are not limited to specific duties. Vertical integration permits staff acceptance of a wide range of responsibilities, which improves morale, increases flexibility in scheduling, establishes a more varied workplace, and builds deeper relationships with residents. An on-call system for nonprofessionals has developed a much better capacity to respond to staffing problems, shortages, illnesses, and other unexpected situations.

This flat management hierarchy works well because Rackleff House is small enough for one supervisor to coordinate staff activities. The initiator of the idea, Keren Brown Wilson, believes it could be successful in facilities of up to sixty residents. Larger facilities might require more than one supervisor. Middle-level management organizational changes would need review to avoid the unwieldy communication lines that could develop. Nevertheless, the concept of vertical integration seems worth considering as an effective management model.

Medicaid Waivers. In terms of financial innovation the success of the Medicaid waiver program as a source of funding the ongoing operation of approximately 40 percent of Rackleff House has depended on the state of Oregon's economy. Funds cannot be expected to remain stable; however, to date the rate of reimbursement is considered adequate and fair. Federal matching funds have remained consistently available, but to control costs at a state level, flexibility in the case management screening of residents for nursing home eligibility has resulted in a redefinition of applicable service-level criteria. As a result, Medicaid recipients assessed at one level can be (and have been) downgraded to a lesser-paying service level.

Recalculated eligibility of residents currently in Rackleff House may continue to result in a reduction of waiver funds available to pay for services. Because this has affected only a few residents, operational funding has not been greatly affected. In larger facilities whose services may range from assisted living to skilled nursing, the gap between Medicaid's pay rate

FIGURE 6.5. *The Paddock Kensington, Beatrice, Nebraska: photo credit Paben Photography*

and actual costs may be considerable. Nevertheless, use of Medicaid waivers, especially in smaller, self-contained assisted living facilities, has been an innovative process for increasing options for the frail, low-income elderly. For states considering implementation of a Medicaid waiver program, the Oregon model offers a successful example that has varied state funding-level caps with client impairment levels.

The Paddock Kensington: Beatrice, Nebraska

Facility Overview

The Paddock Kensington in Beatrice, Nebraska, is a medium-sized, rehabilitated historic hotel serving a primarily rural clientele in a relatively small midwestern town. The sixty-five-room, five-story hotel, built in 1923, is on the National Register of historic buildings, which affords it a significant tax credit. This project is one example of several in which older, elegant hotels have been renovated as assisted living facilities for aging local residents. They are centrally located town markers and are convenient to residents. As a major historic landmark, a center for community activities, and a conventional hotel—in addition to its primary function as an assisted living facility—the Paddock Kensington is a source of pride for its residents and the community.

Innovations in Financing and Management

Tax Credit Developmental Strategy. The Paddock Kensington was developed by the Westin Financial Group as part of its Historic Housing for Seniors (HHS) program. As such it focuses on promoting both investment and social objectives. HHS established a public real estate limited partnership that raised over $10 million in equity to support the concept of acquiring undervalued old hotel properties and renovating them as assisted living housing. Debt financing was minimized and a sound balance between debt and equity financing was established. Conventional financing was obtained for the project at a loan-to-value ratio of approximately 60 percent.

With its basis of $1.549 million in investor equity, the Paddock Kensington Hotel project became eligible for $474,256 in rehabilitation tax credits and $1,689,720 in low-income tax credits. This further reduced project costs while promoting investment objectives. Because it took advantage of low-income tax credits, the project successfully balanced investment objectives with the social objective of providing housing for lower-income elderly residents.

Home Health Agency Service Provision. The entire process is also noteworthy for the creative way it provides assisted living services to residents. To accept tax credits for its development, owners of the project were prohibited from providing their own services. However, for a minimal cost of one dollar per year, a local home health agency rents a storefront office from the hotel and provides residents with personal-care services. Approximately 80 percent of the residents use some home health agency services. An informal weekly evaluation by staff ensures that changes in service need are recognized and addressed when they become evident. A formal assessment by the home health agency schedules services within one-hour increments. Originally, billing for services occurred in fifteen-minute increments; however, once experience proved that longer periods were the service norm, service billing increments expanded to one hour.

Interestingly, in similar assisted living projects developed by the Westin Financial Group, charges from the incremental billing process have proven most competitive where actual costs are the highest. As in other assisted living facilities, residents, their families, and the Paddock Kensington staff cooperate to provide services, thereby reducing costs to individual residents. For example, medications are dispersed at mealtimes. This is supervised by a licensed home health agency nurse and is a service paid for by the Paddock Kensington as part of the general care package.

Supplementary Revenues. In addition, the Paddock Kensington provides its own source of supplementary revenues by renting its large ballroom for community functions. The local high school has used the ballroom for several dances. The increased flow of community members in and out of the building has the added social benefit of mingling generations and creating a stronger community feeling about the building.

Lessons Learned with Potential for External Application

Application of Tax Credits. Although the approach of using tax credits to develop assisted living works in small towns, its successful application to major cities may be more dubious. Higher renovation costs, competition from alternative facilities, and a more transient population all affect small towns much less than large cities. Older areas of major cities are less likely to attract the middle-income resident population than smaller towns. Moreover, as the only five-story building in a town of one- and two-story buildings, assisted living facilities such as the Paddock Kensington are physically prominent. Local residents remember events that occurred in the building years ago and have a commitment to maintain its presence. In a bigger city such ties may be more limited.

Overcoming Target Market Assessment Problems. Like all ventures of this sort, community needs assessment and subsequent marketing form the basis of success. The Paddock Kensington, although beautifully renovated, did not achieve full occupancy as quickly as expected. The region was saturated with senior housing. In addition, the local farming community was hesitant to make the cultural change required to move into town.

To overcome this problem a community educational program was mounted. Paddock Kensington officials met with civic agencies and developed an advisory board to improve public relations with the community. On limited occasions, in the spirit of community exchange, the facility offers vacant rooms to families who are waiting for a home to be completed or to become available for rent. Residents have typically welcomed these families.

Occasionally, rooms are rented to accommodate the overflow from ma-

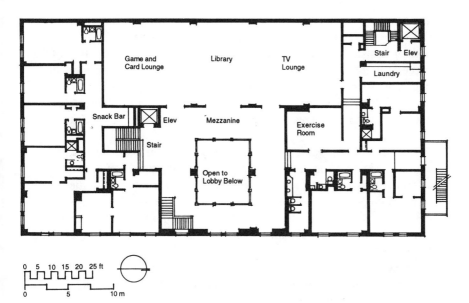

Game and
Card Lounge

Library

TV
Lounge

Stair   Elev

Laundry

Snack Bar   Elev   Mezzanine

Exercise
Room

Stair

Open to
Lobby Below

0 5 10 15 20 25 ft

0   5   10 m

FIGURE 6.6. *Second Floor Plan:* The hotel ballroom was converted to a lounge. Half of the units are studios, the remainder are one and two bedroom units.

jor hotels in town. Efforts have also been made to support the home health agency after availability of in-home services was affected by the facility's opening. Increased communication and the building of a referral network increased the business of both agencies. A flexible rental program allowed residents who needed a larger unit to rent one adjacent to their own and with connecting doors. The strong feeling of community service resulting from increased community interaction has become a primary factor in the success of the Paddock Kensington.

Real Estate Syndicates. In general, real estate syndicates are development driven rather than philosophically inclined. The Westin Financial Group has started twenty-six assisted living facilities in less than three years. Although the Paddock Kensington appears to be a successful example of the general concept of acquiring and adapting undervalued properties for assisted living, there have been financial concerns in other facilities. Success of the concept depends on the market demand for this type of housing. Accurate determination of a target market and the viability of renovating a building are essential elements in determining feasibility.

Operating reserves must also be sufficient during the initial stage. Where attention to these factors is inadequate, projects can lose their focus. One such example resulted in the multipurpose use of a renovated building as both an assisted living facility and a bed-and-breakfast hotel. To be fully successful, management, design, and financing strategies must maintain an integrated focus. The Paddock Kensington has been successful in initiating a mixed-use policy because it developed good communication between agencies and involved residents in supporting a civic-minded endeavor.

Personal-Care Delivery. The Paddock Kensington is also noteworthy in its approach to providing personal care through a contracted home health agency. Similar renovated facilities developed in smaller communities, with limited home-care service, have encountered problems delivering personal-care services at the level desired. It is crucial that potential problems be uncovered during the initial market assessment if any assisted living venture is to succeed.

The Paddock Kensington remains successful because it focuses on providing assisted living in a market that needs it, adapting as changes in the market require adjustment.

Eaton Terrace II: Lakewood, Colorado

Facility Overview

Eaton Terrace II, in Lakewood, Colorado, is a medium-sized nonprofit facility developed for elderly persons with low to middle incomes. Licensed by the state for an occupancy level of seventy-four beds (twenty-one of which are for residents receiving Medicaid) in a six-story, sixty-five-unit building, Eaton Terrace II has remained close to 100 percent occupancy since it opened in December of 1988. At least 92 percent of the facility's resident population has consistently come from the low- to very-low-income groups; only 8 percent have moderate-income status. Steps have been employed to adjust this balance to a 90:10 ratio, with more moderate-income residents offsetting the predominance of low-income residents. Since its opening Eaton Terrace has maintained a waiting list of sixty-five to seventy Medicaid recipients. The unmet demand to service such a resident group has not changed, despite an increased awareness of need.

Innovations in Financing and Management

Developmental Strategy. Eaton Terrace II grew out of a creative request for proposals by the Colorado Housing Authority to develop a pilot assisted living facility for the low-income elderly. As confirmed by our survey, most

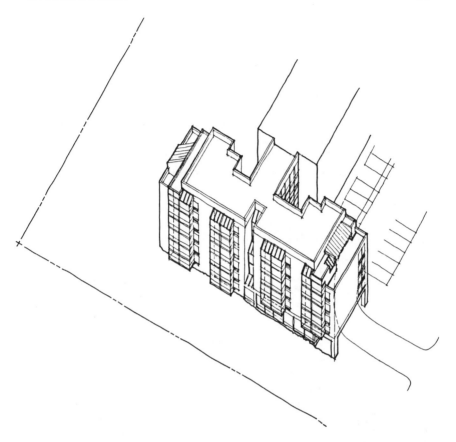

FIGURE 6.7. *Eaton Terrace II, Lakewood, Colorado*

facilities have focused on providing services to a middle- to upper-income population. But as the "aging in place" phenomenon became more apparent in HUD-subsidized congregate housing facilities, the need for assisted living became increasingly evident to Jeffco American Baptist Residences, Inc. Its own facility was experiencing aging in place. Involvement with HUD and its associated restrictions increased the complexity of financing; however, it also offered the potential for innovation in developing Eaton Terrace II.

This facility is integrated programmatically and financially with an HUD congregate housing building on the same property, sponsored by the West Alameda Community Baptist Church (WACBC) and owned by Jeffco American Baptist Residences, Inc. (JABCO). Priority is therefore given to residents of the HUD congregate housing facility whose need for personal services has grown steadily. Priority has also been given to private-pay residents to balance the predominance of low-income residents. Over time many residents spend down their assets and ultimately qualify for Medicaid support.

Eaton Terrace II represents a joint venture between the public and private sectors. HUD underwriting criteria disallowed ownership of both the HUD congregate housing and the assisted living facilities by the same organization. This necessitated the formation of Eaton Terrace II, Inc., a separate corporate entity that obtained a ground lease for the new building.

Financing was structured with the expectation that levels of debt and equity would stay fixed. In retrospect, lower levels of debt would have improved the facility's ability to set future resident rates at a level better suited to carry debt service. A below-market-rate 7 percent loan was obtained through the Colorado Housing Authority, which also guaranteed a small second trust deed for which interest-only payments continue for approximately fifteen years. WACBC subsidized the remaining cost through a $55,000 equity contribution.

Targeting Low-Income Elderly Using Medicaid Payments. With a philosophy based on support of low-income elderly, Eaton Terrace II faced HUD restrictions on occupancy:

- Twenty percent was required to house the very low-income elderly whose annual income, including income from assets and 5.5 percent of nonperforming assets, amounted to less than $13,850/
- Twenty percent was reserved for the low-income elderly with a $22,160 annual income cap.
- Sixty percent was allowed to be available for moderate-income elderly with a $33,240 annual income cap.

When the facility opened, a consistent occupancy pattern developed, with only 8 percent of the residents falling in the moderate-income category, whereas 57 percent remained in the very-low-income category. The following efforts have improved this ratio somewhat; however, Eaton Terrace II remains committed to continuing the effort, to sustain its own financial viability.

Like Rackleff House, the Eaton Terrace II financing process is particularly noteworthy as an example of preserving the affordability of rental housing for low-income elderly through use of Medicaid-funded payments for assisted living services. Eligibility in Colorado for this state assistance

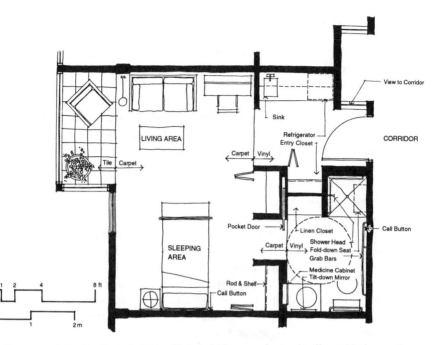

FIGURE 6.8. *Studio unit:* This efficient 345 square foot unit offers a kitchen, private bathroom and a small tiled alcove that can be used for plants or furniture.

under the Alternative Care Facility program is determined by a state-appointed social worker, but selection criteria are flexibly based on state-controlled caps in Medicaid waiver funding and the number of persons served.

Currently, the rent and services of approximately fourteen residents at Eaton Terrace II are subsidized through the Medicaid waiver program. Reimbursement amounts to $772 per month, which is a slight increase over prior years because of an SSI adjustment added to stabilize state levels. This compares with a tiered private payment range of $1,180 to $1,854 based on varying unit sizes. Although very modest incremental gains have boosted the Medicaid reimbursement rate in past years, it continues to be approximately $100 to $150 below actual costs. This fact, combined with the resident bias toward the very-low-income elderly, necessitated the employment of several cost-containing management strategies to balance the low-income and self-paying resident mix better and to improve cash flow.

- Total costs to residents rose over the past three years from a base of $939 to $1,180 (a 25 percent increase), with the cap rising from $1,613 to $1,854 (a 15 percent increase). The administration now believes that rates are where they need to be to ensure adequate cash flow and expects them to hold level in 1993.
- Operating costs have been cut through better allocation of staffing and meal costs between the neighboring HUD congregate housing facility and Eaton Terrace II, combined with a rebid of the bulk insurance package. Despite general increases in costs, labor costs have remained low as a result of reduced staff turnover. Changes in scheduling have benefited both staff and residents, to reduce absentee and sick rates.
- Medicaid reimbursement residents have been assessed, matched, and in some cases encouraged to accept a double-occupancy tenancy arrangement. Currently, seven units have two occupants, more than administrators would like to see to maintain resident independence and privacy. However, the L-shaped design of rooms for two occupants minimizes the impact to residents.
- Operating reserves have been gradually built to higher levels than were originally anticipated to be necessary. (The originally estimated $150,000 reserve pool should have been doubled.)

Lessons Learned with Potential for External Application

Equity to Loan Balance for Low-income Resident Base. Because the target market was low-income elderly, fewer equity dollars were available to limit future debt service costs. Financial analyses of Eaton Terrace II determined that a 60 percent equity payment would have enabled rental rates to carry the debt service. In retrospect, state agencies would have better served the sponsor and the low-income elderly they support by contributing equity to this project and projects like it. This would increase the feasibility of projects serving low-income populations and enable them to carry their debt service.

Despite continued cash flow difficulties, Eaton Terrace II has been successful, demonstrating that housing oriented solely toward a low-income population can be financially viable. In an environment focused on maximizing the independence of each resident, resident functionality has improved more than expected. Each year between 5 and 10 percent of the resident population moves to a more independent setting.

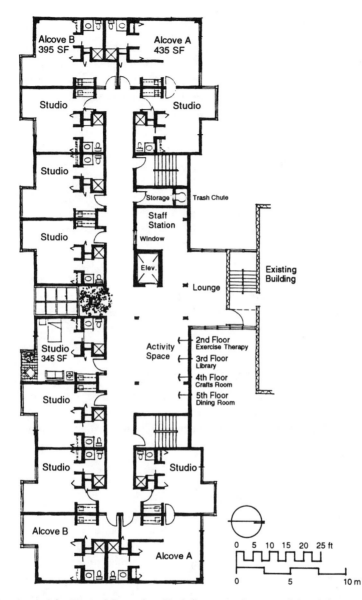

Alcove B
395 SF

Alcove A
435 SF

Studio

Studio

Studio

Studio

Storage   Trash Chute

Staff
Station

Window

Elev.

Lounge

Existing
Building

Activity
Space

2nd Floor
Exercise Therapy

3rd Floor
Library

4th Floor
Crafts Room

5th Floor
Dining Room

Studio
345 SF

Studio

Studio

Studio

Alcove B

Alcove A

0 5 10 15 20 25 ft

0   5   10 m

FIGURE 6.9. *Typical floor plan:* Each floor contains a special activity space. The second floor lounge is used for exercise, the third floor is a library, the fourth floor is a crafts room, and the fifth floor is a double height dining room.

Marketing Strategy. Marketing for the facility promotes the concept of restoring resident functionality in an effort to reach potential residents before they experience severe functional decline. Such benefits from an assisted living environment are most evident when residents stay for an extended period in the early stages of functional loss.

Shift Scheduling Strategy. As with other comprehensive assisted living facilities, difficulties have arisen in supporting residents with acute levels of dysfunction. Although only 10 to 15 percent of the resident population falls into this category, they can disrupt other residents. Their need for higher levels of service can impinge on staff availability to other residents and therefore increase staff stress levels. To avoid related staff problems, administrators implemented an innovative scheduling change.

In each twenty-four-hour period, shifts changed from three- to eight-hour to two- to twelve-hour intervals. Staff members work twelve hours on three consecutive days, followed by four days off. This program provides thirty-six hours of work time each week, although staff members are compensated for forty hours. In exchange, staff can be called upon to work an extra four-hour shift when necessary; however, most average only one or two such shifts each month.

Problems of burnout, absenteeism, staff sickness, and turnover have been reduced, and employees find that their ability to meet their own family day-care needs has improved. Residents have also benefited from the continuity of staff members who have become familiar with their total daily needs. This change has benefited everyone and avoided increases in labor costs.

Balancing Low-Income and Private-Pay Resident Mix. From a financial standpoint, Eaton Terrace II has taken advantage of multiple funding options, both public and private, to enhance its economic feasibility. Before the facility opened, seventy-five elderly were waitlisted for Medicaid-subsidized units. This figure has changed little in the four years of operation. As a result of the program's effectiveness in keeping frail residents out of a nursing home, turnover rates have remained very low in the subsidized units.

Those elderly on the waiting list often find themselves choosing a nursing home, at a cost to the state of 20 percent more than that of assisted living. By the time a unit becomes available at Eaton Terrace II, many older people on the waiting list experience a functional decline that makes them ineligible for placement in assisted living. Eaton Terrace administration estimates a $5,000 annual savings to Medicaid could occur for each person who must be placed in a nursing home setting because assisted living is unavailable. Nothing in this study has suggested that similar savings do not apply elsewhere.

Attracting an economically viable balance of low-income and self-paying residents remains a key management problem. As noted, strategies that increase proportions of self-paying residents and reduce the number of very-low-income elderly can be expected to increase cash flow without affecting quality of service. However, new rate structures, which were expected to aggravate the problem of limited availability of assisted living units for low-income elderly, have not changed the balance of residents at Eaton Terrace II.

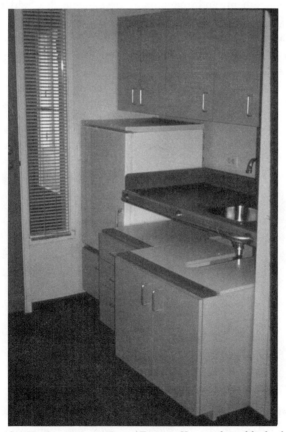

FIGURE 6.10. *Kitchen units at Eaton Terrace II are adaptable for handicapped users:* A side window also links the galley kitchen to the corridor.

Need for Public Subsidy. Eaton Terrace II provides an example of a successful innovative-financing pilot. It not only demonstrates the urgent need for long-term federal and state initiatives to subsidize the increased numbers of low-income elderly in assisted living housing, but also suggests the need to advocate for reliable third-party payment sources to increase the residential options for the frail.

Woodside Place: Oakmont, Pennsylvania

Facility Overview

Woodside Place in Oakmont, Pennsylvania, exemplifies a medium-sized, stand-alone assisted living facility that combines extensive innovations in design, management, and financing to serve the needs of elderly dementia residents. Opened in July 1991, its three single-story houses accommodate thirty-six residents. From the very beginning, Woodside Place has maintained an occupancy rate of almost 100 percent, with a waiting list of sixty people at most times. It represents the culmination of a highly researched, well-planned and coordinated cooperative venture between multiple public and private agencies.

FIGURE **6.11.** *Woodside Place, Oakmont, Pennsylvania*

Innovations in Financing and Management Approach

Public/Private Partnership Developmental Strategy. Woodside Place emphasizes the effectiveness of establishing a public/private partnership to maximize resources available for the development and ongoing operation of an assisted living facility. It serves a substantial low-income elderly population and is the first such facility with a systematic, case-controlled study of its care program. All organizations involved have a professional and financial stake in the project's success. The sponsors have focused on filling a continuum-of-care gap in southwestern Pennsylvania's Allegheny County. They anticipate that state agencies interested in economic alternatives to nursing homes will find convincing evidence for lower cost of care in this assisted living setting.

It is hoped that the success of this project will encourage state agencies to support the ongoing financing of assisted living in Pennsylvania. Clinical data will permit comparisons with more institutional nursing home environments with respect to the impact of assisted living on the progression of Alzheimer's disease (AD), behavioral and social manifestations of the disease, staff and family satisfaction, resident and staff turnover, and staff training needs. The primary research goal is to quantify quality-of-life issues and episodes of positive interaction in a residential versus an institutional setting.

Well-Researched Concept. The idea behind Woodside Place began in 1988 when the Presbyterian Association on Aging (PAOA) and the Western Pennsylvania Hospital (WPH) joined forces to conduct an investigation of assisted living alternatives to nursing home placement. The resulting eighteen-month study was funded by a $100,000 endowment from the Howard Heinz Foundation awarded jointly to PAOA and WPH to identify gaps in the continuum of care for older persons. After recognition of the high numbers of sufferers of AD in the local community and after a review of care settings around the world, the design of Woodside Place began.

Through its development and construction stages Woodside Place was financed by a variety of public and private resources. An advisory committee was developed with representation from many agencies and foundations that had contributed to the project's funding. However, those involved incorporated the expertise of consultants (including M. Powell Lawton) to ensure that the project design and concept remained practical. Attention to detail from the very beginning resulted in a facility whose design has won

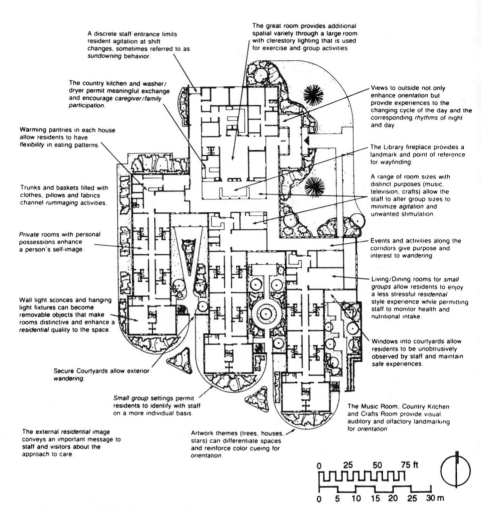

A discrete staff entrance limits resident agitation at shift changes, sometimes referred to as *sundowning* behavior.

The country kitchen and washer/dryer permit meaningful exchange and encourage *caregiver/family participation*.

Warming pantries in each house allow residents to have *flexibility* in eating patterns.

Trunks and baskets filled with clothes, pillows and fabrics channel *rummaging* activities.

Private rooms with personal possessions enhance a person's self-image.

Wall light sconces and hanging light fixtures can become removable objects that make rooms distinctive and enhance a *residential* quality to the space.

Secure Courtyards allow exterior *wandering*.

Small group settings permit residents to identify with staff on a more individual basis.

The external *residential* image conveys an important message to staff and visitors about the approach to care.

Artwork themes (trees, houses, stars) can differentiate spaces and reinforce color cueing for *orientation*.

The great room provides additional spatial variety through a large room with clerestory lighting that is used for exercise and group activities.

Views to outside not only enhance *orientation* but provide experiences to the changing cycle of the day and the corresponding *rhythms* of night and day.

The Library fireplace provides a landmark and point of reference for *wayfinding*.

A range of room sizes with distinct purposes (music, television, crafts) allow the staff to alter group sizes to minimize *agitation* and unwanted stimulation.

Events and activities along the corridors give purpose and interest to *wandering*.

Living/Dining rooms for *small groups* allow residents to enjoy a less stressful *residential* style experience while permitting staff to monitor health and nutritional intake.

Windows into courtyards allow residents to be unobtrusively observed by staff and maintain *safe* experiences.

The Music Room, Country Kitchen and Crafts Room provide visual, auditory and olfactory landmarking for *orientation*.

0   25   50   75 ft

0   5   10   15   20   25   30 m

FIGURE 6.12. *Floor plan:* The corridor that connects the three bungalow houses to common activity spaces is used extensively by wanderers. Special rooms have been designed for activities such as music, crafts, TV viewing, family socializing and exercising.

numerous awards for the architects, Perkins-Eastman and Partners of New York City. It exemplifies an environment that effectively combines residential, therapeutic, and prosthetic qualities to promote independence and dignity.

Since PAOA owned the site on which it planned to build Woodside Place, it focused on securing funding by mobilizing financial resources from many organizations. Eighteen different private foundations of national and local prominence invested $1.6 million in development efforts. An additional $200,000 grant was obtained from the Allegheny County Housing Development Corporation, and the state of Pennsylvania's Housing Finance Agency contributed $300,000. The latter also covered the remaining balance of debt with a $589,000 loan obtained through tax-exempt bonds.

Low-Income Resident Subsidy. Through this financing of capital costs, Woodside Place is committed to serving a resident base comprised of 50 percent low-income residents. At least four residents receive SSI supplements approximating $600 per month. These and the remaining low-income residents are subsidized by the PAOA at a reduced rate of $50 per day to cover actual costs. The remaining private-pay daily rate of $86 for private and $82 for semiprivate rooms offsets the cash flow reduction from low-income residents. To ensure financial privacy, only the administrator knows the residents who belong in various financial categories.

Based on an anticipated average occupancy rate of 95 percent, Woodside Place has been a break-even operation. With a constant waiting list and an occupancy rate approaching 100 percent, rooms are rarely available. In fact, the waiting list represents at least a two-year list of potential residents at all times. When room vacancies arise, admissions staff typically find that two or three people on the waiting list have deteriorated past the point at which they can be accepted into the program.

Financial viability of the facility is enhanced through the continued attention of both the PAOA and WPH to funding of low-income resident subsidies, and the essential program evaluation and training components of the study. The PAOA is committed to supporting ongoing operational costs of $750,000 annually, approximately 66 percent of which are covered by the private-pay residents.

Long-term-care insurance companies have regularly refused to support residents of Woodside Place because it does not precisely fit their criteria for Medicare certification. Together, these factors leave 34 percent of costs to be funded through SSI payments, PAOA-subsidized rentals, grants, and other charitable contributions. The PAOA and WPH are also currently pursuing the funding of their three-year Woodside Place evaluation, through grants.

Associated Research Component. Woodside Place is expected to provide state agencies with evidence that shows the cost savings of providing care through assisted living as an alternative to a nursing home. As part of the study, one-third of the initial residents were moved from a nursing home where daily rates were ninety-nine dollars. The private-pay rate for residents of Woodside Place is nearly 20 percent less than the cost of nursing home care. Moreover, the philosophy of Woodside Place promotes independence and maximum functionality.

Recognizing the potential for cost-effectively responding to needs of a vulnerable elderly population, Woodside Place has been developed with innovation and quality in mind rather than just cost. It has therefore become a test site for demonstrating success in alternative design, management, and financing philosophies.

Lessons Learned with Potential for External Application

Public/Private Partnership. Success of the public/private joint venture to establish Woodside Place hinges primarily on the depth of the complementary expertise of the parties involved and their emphasis on a charitable financial model. Successful financial control and management depend primarily on the PAOA, which is both the owner and the operator. However, this is coupled with expertise in senior-care program development offered by WPH, a research and teaching facility, whose director of geriatric medicine has been appointed medical director to Woodside Place.

The administrator of the facility is affiliated with both the PAOA and WPH through a matrix management structure, which maximizes communication between the agencies. Based on their recognized long-term commitment to meeting health and social needs of the elderly, the PAOA and WPH present an impressive team with complementary credentials. Other projects with a similar commitment to market analysis and planning should expect similar results.

Impact of AD on Service Philosophy. Unlike the "ideal" assisted living environment detailed earlier in this book, Woodside Place does not promote the concept of caring for residents within the facility until they die. Residents must therefore remain ambulatory and continent to avoid transfer. Although the Woodside Place environment encourages maximum functioning

FIGURE 6.13. *The great room at Woodside is used for exercise classes and group activities:* Light enters the room from clerestory windows. The quilts throughout the building were custom designed for decorative and orientation purposes.

for as long as possible, the progression of AD increases a resident's need for personal service. Although intolerance of the manifestations of advancing disease is understandable, alternatives to institutional transfer are being tested elsewhere (e.g., Rosewood Estate), to maximize the quality of life of all residents until death. It is hoped that this practice will be encouraged at Woodside Place in the future.

Unexpected Design Problem. An unexpected surprise resulted from the prominent placement of the front door. This typical residential feature is very distracting to the cognitively impaired residents of Woodside Place. Because of its visibility residents often try to exit the building and become frustrated when they are unsuccessful. Environmental design considerations for those with dementia must recognize such potential problems despite their obvious benefit in terms of residential imagery.

Demonstrated Cost Savings. The demonstrated success of Woodside Place in achieving cost savings has increased public interest in this area. Although Woodside Place focuses on serving residents whose frailty and vulnerability are attributable to AD, the same approach can be expected to apply to other frail, vulnerable, and low-income elderly. In an economic climate of restricted funding options, use of such project-based public and private partnerships offers an innovative approach to financing the development of assisted living. Applications of such concepts can be expected to expand, especially if ventures like Woodside Place would prove successful.

Rosewood Estate: Roseville, Minnesota

Facility Overview

Rosewood Estate in Roseville, Minnesota, is an example of a medium-sized facility that employs extensive innovations in design, management, and financing to serve very frail elderly. As a three-story unlicensed facility, opened in September 1989, Rosewood Estate has a capacity of sixty-eight residential units serving a suburban community in a self-contained assisted living environment. The facility focuses on serving middle- and upper-income elderly whose only care option is that of a nursing home. Surprisingly, 50 percent of the residents moved from nursing home settings and 13 percent came from hospitals. Rosewood Estate now has almost a 100 percent occupancy rate. With a philosophy that strongly supports managed risk and encourages practicality in offering care, residents remain as functionally independent as possible.

Innovations in Financing and Management

Developmental Strategy: HUD Financing. Rosewood Estate was developed as one of the last facilities to use HUD 221(d)4 retirement center financing, a source of funding that ended during the HUD crisis of the late 1980s. However, the financing arrangement for ensuring home health services proved useful.

FIGURE 6.14. *Rosewood Estate, Roseville, Minnesota.*

Personal-Care Service Provision. As in many assisted living facilities, an in-house home health agency provides personal-care services to residents of Rosewood Estate. Services are controlled and defined on an individual basis, determined through a multidisciplinary assessment of residents before their admission to the facility and every six months (or less) after occupancy.

Quality of care is maintained through a case management process that coordinates home health workers, Rosewood staff, residents, and their family. Full-time registered nurses representing the home health agency and Rosewood Estate coordinate service delivery. Aided by a computerized care management system that connects formal and informal providers, they author a twenty-four-hour care plan that encourages family interaction. The outcome is increased independence for residents and their families, who also feel part of the care system.

Tailored services are accounted for in fifteen-minute increments, at a cost of $5.35 per increment. This preserves the affordability of services, since payment is required only for services received. In fact, 20 percent of

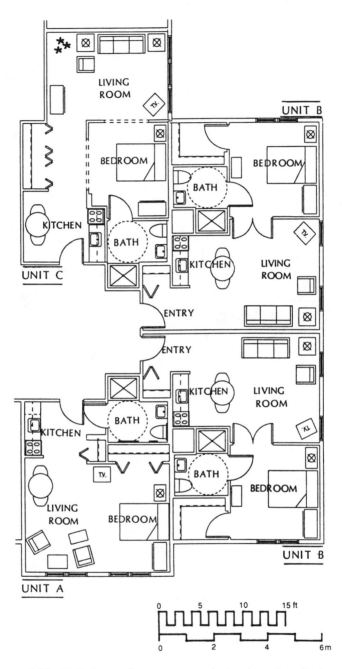

Figure 6.15. *Unit cluster:* Four rooms are clustered together. Each contains a kitchen and bathroom with enough space for a dining room table, an easy chair and a bed.

the current residents do not maintain any contract with the home health agency for any services. On occasion they may request help, but for the majority of their personal needs they remain independent. Service contracts range from a need for no services to a need for twelve increments daily.

The average cost is about twenty dollars per day. (Lifeline emergency response is available twenty-four hours daily to all residents as part of their standard monthly lease.) Since opening, a limited packaged approach has developed for some services (e.g., medications and laundry). Recently, a new escort service package providing up to eight escorts per day was offered for $200 per month. This has become an attractive packaged service for the four residents suffering from dementia who are otherwise relatively independent.

Sophisticated Computerized Care Management System. To support the ideal of care as a service rather than a procedure, a computer care management system distributes personalized care plans to formal home health agency providers and Rosewood Estate staff. Information provided from the point of service includes housekeeping, medications, DNR orders, newspaper delivery requests, and other individual details of the general care plan that complement demographic and medical history data. In addition, a further marketing component of the system tracks prospective residents, referrals, and leads, enabling faster response as facility vacancies arise. This computer system has been refined from its initial implementation at Elder-Homestead, in Minnetonka, Minnesota, and may have application elsewhere in other, similar facilities.

Prototype Agreement with Home Health Agency. To ensure that personal services were available to residents needing them when the facility first opened, a prototype agreement was reached between the home health agency and Rosewood Estate. The need to remain sensitive to the difficulties of maintaining adequate cash flow while establishing a reliable client base was recognized. In exchange for provision of twenty-four-hour services by the home health agency, Rosewood Estate provided space and utilities, in addition to a subsidy to guarantee financial security during start-up operations. The subsidy derived from determining the cost of one staff person twenty-four hours per day for a month, a total of $5,000.

Operationally, the agency collected a dollar subsidized offset for every dollar of revenue they collected, to the guaranteed floor of $5,000. After three months in operation, the agency reached its $5,000 revenue level but recognized an increased need for additional support. Acknowledging the increasing costs to the agency because of increasing facility occupancy and needs, Rosewood Estate renegotiated its agreement and increased its guaranteed subsidy floor to $10,000. In practice, it paid this guaranteed subsidy only during the start-up operation. In the following year, 1991, no associated financial outlay was made. The facility filled in 11.5 months and has maintained an occupancy rate of close to 100 percent.

Philosophy of Managed Risk. Most residents that choose to maximize their independence bear a responsibility for increased vulnerability. Rosewood Estate operates within a philosophical framework that supports managed risk, a philosophy also promoted at Rackleff House. In the course of each individual's evaluation, levels of prudent and reasonable risk are established with agreement from family members, residents, and staff. However, if behavioral or physical changes occur that make a resident unsafe, the staff members intervene to establish a more appropriate level of risk.

For those with Alzheimer's disease this has been an especially successful program, managing the generally challenging problems associated with dementia. To date, residents have not exhibited abusive or aggressive behaviors, but twenty-four-hour protective oversight does manage their wandering behavior successfully. Practicality remains the overriding factor, so that policies and procedures, staff, residents, and family members remain flexible in their approach to care.

Lessons Learned with Potential for External Application

Care as Service. A major factor in the success of Rosewood Estate appears to be the diligent acceptance of the facility's philosophy of care by staff, residents, their families, and the home health agency. Care is very specific and very personalized. As much as possible, all involved take a practical approach to service delivery by minimizing rigidity. As a result, residents have often been able to live out their lives in dignity in this residential environment.

Annual turnover has approximated 65 percent; the bulk of these residents either die or return home with family members. Close to 30 percent have required a discharge to a nursing home because of problem behaviors resulting from advanced dementia, or as a result of spending so many of their assets that they can no longer afford rental payments. The goal, however, remains focused on providing a home for residents until they die or can move to a more independent living arrangement.

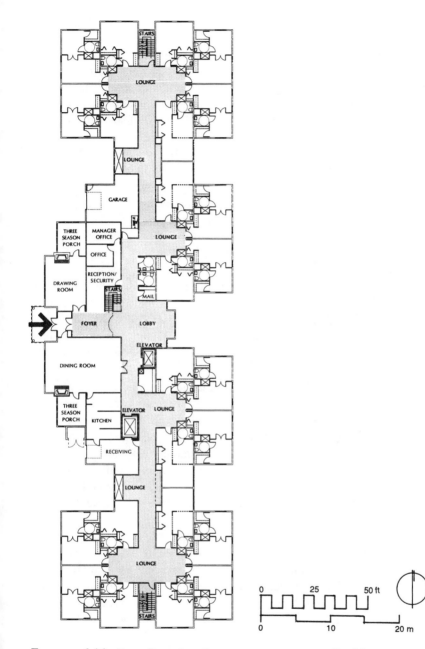

FIGURE 6.16. *Entry floor plan:* Common spaces are centralized for easy access near the entry. Views toward the east are of an adjacent lake.

Home Health Agency Start-Up. Success in providing assisted living services to residents of Rosewood Estate was ensured by guaranteeing the income of the home health agency during the critical operational start-up. Based on the premise that a good home health agency would not ultimately lose money with an established client base, Rosewood Estate marketed its service provision partnership to all potential residents. Such a subsidy could be considered a cost of marketing, a cost probably bearable only by a middle- to upper-income resident population. In hindsight, enticing the home health agency through the subsidy seems unnecessary, since both the Rosewood Estate facility and the home health agency were committed to providing high-quality care.

Future assisted living projects planning to provide care through a coordinated home health agency agreement may find that an interest-free loan would suffice to initiate a successful venture. However, the creative prototypical approach tested by Rosewood Estate may still be most effective in selective situations. With the added assurance of an on-site registered nurse as a full-time part of the staff (something Rosewood Estate would add if they were to repeat the process and have since added), facility marketing can focus on the availability of services across a very wide spectrum of need.

Incremental Service Billing. Success of the incremental approach to billing services was criticized by a number of other facility administrators during the course of our study. For some resident needs, fifteen-minute increments were believed to be financially prohibitive; walking assistance to and from the dining room, for example, would initially have cost $10 for two fifteen-minute increments, although each trip did not usually consume its full time increment. Administrators who were critical suggested that such an arrangement discouraged residents from seeking minimal levels of needed assistance.

The alternative to billing in service increments, that of providing selected service packages to residents, was considered at Rosewood but has been implemented to only a limited degree. Individual needs are being well met, and informal assistance is encouraged; therefore the packaging of major services has not been considered an issue. Packaging services seems most appropriate for such specialized services as escorting, medications, and laundry.

Partnership Approach to Service Provision. At Rosewood Estate the key to maintaining appropriate levels of service is the ongoing case management process of regular reassessment. If services are deemed necessary, residents are discouraged from opting out during the negotiation of the service contract, which provides the basis for the daily computerized care report.

Of major importance to meeting resident needs is the encouragement of family and neighbor cooperation in providing as many services as possible. Residents help each other to the dining rooms, and families are encouraged to participate as much as they can. Daily changes can be made to the computer system to accommodate minor changes in service needs without inconveniencing staff, families, or residents. In this way, highly personalized billable service levels are maintained at a minimum for each resident, preserving their perceived and actual independence as long as possible.

Transition to Alternative Care Facilities. A further transition may be necessary if a resident can no longer afford to live here. To date, only a few individuals have had to be transferred to a nursing home for financial reasons. The first resident to be faced with a spend-down problem was moved to a smaller efficiency unit, Medicaid supplements were invoked, but in exchange for his considerable on-site volunteer service, Rosewood Estate subsidized his rent until he was unable to stay for other reasons. Each case is treated on its merits; nevertheless, for any viable for-profit organization, heavy facility-based subsidies cannot become a regular occurrence.

Lincolnia Center: Fairfax, Virginia

Facility Overview

Lincolnia Center in Fairfax, Virginia, is a twenty-six-unit (double-occupied) assisted living facility for fifty-two residents, developed on the second floor of a three-story building. Community facilities are available at the same site in an adjoining adaptively reused elementary school. The assisted living facility serves as a component of a diverse services complex, combining a senior center with community facilities and low-income housing for an elderly population in varying stages of dependency. It models the European "service house" approach to supporting resident and community needs.

This project follows a prototype completed by Fairfax County in the 1980s with minimal funds for building rehabilitation. Lincolnia Center expanded on this concept, and as part of the total school rehabilitation represents the transformation of a neighborhood eyesore into a useful local resource.

FIGURE 6.17. *Lincolnia Center, Fairfax, Virginia*

Innovations in Financing and Management

Public Partnership. Lincolnia Center was developed through a project-based public partnership of multiple Fairfax County agencies that represent a broad public constituency. Total cost for renovation of the 57,000-square-foot recreational center and the construction of the building for independent apartments and assisted living was $8 million.

To take advantage of the existing but unused elementary school, the Fairfax County Housing Authority obtained a 100-year land lease from the local school board for one dollar per year. Technically, this allows the school board to retain ownership of the site without giving up title to the land, although the Fairfax County Housing Authority retains ownership and management responsibilities. Financing of the building renovation and construction of the three-story assisted living and independent housing were obtained through local general funds. No direct federal funding was made available.

Among those local agencies involved in coordinating the wide variety of programs are the local Area Agency on Aging, Department of Human Development, Department of Recreation and Community Services, Health Department, and Community Services Board. They maintain specific roles as members of this public partnership. Such a partnership of government service providers, with differing agendas, had never been attempted in the county before and was initially met with some trepidation. At first the concept was awkward, since it was new to assisted living and to the agencies involved; however, a team approach has now developed with clear roles assigned to each agency, coordinated by the Fairfax County Housing Authority.

European Community-Minded Service House Approach. County authorities have been highly impressed with the unique way agencies successfully work together. This partnership is enhanced by the residents and members of the community as well. Lincolnia Center offers a community feel to its campus. Its senior recreation center is considered the most active in the county in terms of the population served, programs offered, and general community acceptance. Increased mingling of community members with those of the assisted living facility also enhances the social effectiveness of the arrangement, increasing resident perceptions of independence.

Residents of the third-floor independent housing units volunteer at the Adult Day Health center. The convenient attached housing also encourages more disabled residents to participate in senior center activities. Volunteers from the community regularly support programs, including an intergenerational relationship with a local elementary school. Lincolnia Center residents of varying functional levels visit elementary school classes, and students also come to the center and the Adult Day Health program. The experience for both students and residents is positive, educational, and effective in building tolerant, sensitive, and caring relationships between generations.

In addition to the six local agencies involved, Lincolnia Center has contracted with Sunrise Retirement Homes to manage the assisted living facility. Sunrise is paid for management and food service on a twenty-four-hour basis, seven days per week. The contract is renewed annually, but covers a three-year proposal period.

Low-Income Resident Population. Resident priority is given to people with very low annual incomes. No one with an annual income currently greater than $17,850 can apply for housing. In assisted living, state Department of Social Services subsidies are provided on an individual basis, calculated as a function of income. Auxiliary grant payments of $725 per month are paid for those eligible. If residents have a monthly income of more than $700 and therefore do not qualify for auxiliary payments, they pay 60 percent of their income for living in the facility, including shelter, food, supervision, and service needs. The remaining 40 percent of their income goes

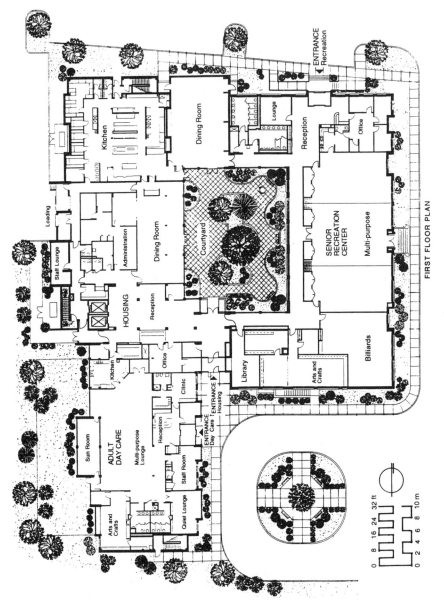

FIGURE 6.18. *The Lincolnia site plan shows multiple uses surrounding the centralized courtyard:* These include a senior center, independent housing, assisted living and an adult day care center.

toward medical and personal needs. The general county fund subsidizes the shortfall for all assisted living residents.

Since the population served in the assisted living facility is primarily very low income, Lincolnia Center is especially noteworthy for the innovative way in which personal-care services are economically provided. The alternative housing option for most of these elderly remains a nursing home or transfer to an affordable facility in far-out rural Virginia. It has not been surprising therefore to see a continued list of seventy-five to eighty people waiting an average of nine months to one year for an available space. For 75 percent of these potential residents, care needs dictate a more supportive setting by the time they have permission to move. Clearly, a substantial need exists for additional assisted living services to support a low-income frail population in the county.

Lessons Learned with Potential for External Application

Need for Clear Role Definition. Although the approach of using a public partnership of agencies to provide assisted living services for low-income elderly seems obvious, there are some drawbacks. Such a committee design can uncover competing agency rules, regulations, or institutional constraints that block the process of cost-effective project development. For example, the Health Department and Community Services Board was tied to a medical model that conflicted with the residential model most appropriate for an assisted living philosophy. When agency roles are defined at project inception, problems resulting from perceived goal conflicts can be identified and minimized. In the long run, the advantage of using available expertise within existing government services outweighs the potential for problems.

In the case of Lincolnia Center, most problems have been resolved by clearly establishing agency participation levels and bringing all parties together in a concerted team approach that effectively uses services provided by each agency. It seems apparent that more housing authorities could model this European service house, public partnership approach to providing assisted living to those very-low-income elderly in need.

Compromises Due to Limited Funding. Providing assisted living for a low-income population continues to be difficult, despite community and agency support. Although Lincolnia Center's philosophy is to keep residents independent as long as possible, those whose physical or medical needs are more serious must unfortunately be transferred to a nursing home. Cost-effective balancing of staffing levels to maintain financial viability requires very close monitoring and budgetary scrutiny. Funding is not available to increase staffing levels as a resident's needs increase. Incontinence alone does not necessitate resident transfer; however, behavioral disruption and/or mental or physical decline that renders residents mostly unable to care for themselves leaves Lincolnia Center with no choice but to transfer residents.

With a long waiting list, occupancy rates stay high, approximating 100 percent. A cooperative admissions program ensures that this continues. The Interagency Admissions and Discharge Team, an outgrowth of continuing agency planning and strategizing, consults with family members, social workers, and members of the Lincolnia and Sunrise staffs to ascertain resident appropriateness for admission or discharge. As an existing resident continues to decline, the team prepares both the resident and his or her family for an anticipated transfer while completing the screening of a replacement. Although this is a difficult task, it works because those affected by decisions are involved in the process.

Accommodating Frailty. Of surprise to both agencies and staff members has been the level of tolerant interaction between fully independent and highly frail residents. Much of this seems to result from placing independent residents directly above the assisted living facility. The original assumption that each would be separate has never been true. Although residents in the independent units have become frail and moved down to the assisted living facility as expected, a major surprise has been the movement of residents from assisted living to the increased levels of independence on the third floor. This movement and voluntary interaction at the Adult Health Care facility encourage stimulating social exchange among residents of varying levels of frailty.

In addition, as a result, segregation of residents at mealtimes has proven totally unnecessary. When the building first opened, one evening meal seating serviced the independent units and another serviced the assisted living facility. Residents themselves ignored this plan and all ate together. As the building filled, the split seating arrangement was recommended again. Residents generally did not see the need, however, and continued to enjoy taking meals together. In retrospect it seems that resident tolerance of frailty was much higher than expected, a situation that has served to educate staff and reaffirm the importance of upholding and fostering values of tolerance, independence, dignity, and individuality.

FIGURE 6.19. *Sunrise of Frederick, Frederick, Maryland*

Sunrise of Frederick: Frederick, Maryland

Facility Overview

Sunrise of Frederick, in Frederick, Maryland, exemplifies a medium-sized facility, privately financed by a foreign equity investment with a conventional bank loan, combining extensive design, management, and philosophical innovations. Following the commitment to maximizing the quality of life of the frail and vulnerable elderly that has been the hallmark of Sunrise for at least the past ten years, Frederick serves a bedroom community of Baltimore and Washington, D.C., in the center of the county. A three-story facility opened in March 1992, Frederick maintains a capacity of sixty residential units in a self-contained setting, accommodating seventy-two residents as a result of twelve double-occupancy units for low-income residents. It illustrates the continued Sunrise commitment to superior care by adapting prior models based on the experiences of currently operating facilities.

Innovations in Financing and Management Approach

Conservative Financing with Foreign Investment. In a small town about an hour from Washington, D.C., Frederick represents the first Sunrise retirement home constructed outside a suburban setting. It joins ten other Sunrise homes in the general northern Virginia and southern Maryland region.

Although no "cookie cutter" approach to financing development is practiced, Frederick follows the typically conservative approach taken by Sunrise in general. Although tax-exempt bonds, HUD programs, taxable bonds, REITs, and other tools have been assessed, traditional bank loans have been determined to be the easiest and most reliable method of financing. Frederick was therefore financed through an 80 percent conventional bank loan, with a five- to seven-year floating rate, and a 20 percent cash equity payment. Unit development costs for Frederick—including working capital reserves, interest reserve, land, construction, and other extraneous costs—approximate $100,000, the Sunrise standard.

Asian investors provided the cash investment. Although the industry has become used to long-term investments, Asian venture capitalists are changing the perspective on private facility development. Although willing to accept risks, their attitude is one of maximizing short-term gain, expecting a 30 to 40 percent return. As sophisticated investors, they therefore require

- Deep discounts, obtainable generally through noncash equity.
- A typical investment duration of two, five, or ten years maximum.
- Known risk, as a result of real estate debt already established.

Although Frederick is a newly constructed facility, responding to the requirements of Asian investors will most probably encourage the current Sunrise program of upgrading acquisitions to fit their assisted living model. The recent economic downturn appears to have established this as a trend in the housing industry. Continued new construction might be expected to involve wealthy individuals, private corporations, utility companies, and other domestic investors, as in the past, but to a lesser degree. To limit complexity, Sunrise typically retains only one equity investor per project.

Construction Deviations. In an effort to preclude retroactive construction costs in the future, Frederick was built to nursing home I-2 construction standards. In the past two years, increased education and evidence of the importance of a more homelike environment in meeting needs of the frail elderly seem to have somewhat averted this trend, so that in retrospect such construction rigidity may not have been necessary. However, in terms of long-term durability and in support of highly dysfunctional residents, Frederick is well prepared. Conforming to I-2 standards incurred an extra cost of four to five dollars a square foot. Moreover, it accommodated potential regulations stemming from the Sunrise desire to allow residents to age in place in their facilities and eventually die there. However, despite the I-2 construction standards, residential design priorities do not appear to have been severely compromised.

Success in meeting budgeted goals for Frederick was an important factor, especially considering the expectations of Asian investors. However, after developers broke ground and problems occurred with foundation footings, an additional $100,000 became necessary to correct the problems. Cost savings were achieved by modifying the HVAC system and the other features, but not at the expense of ensuring a homelike environment for residents. In fact, as a result of careful adjustments, facility quality was barely affected, and the original $100,000 was gained back by the end of construction. Anticipation of obstacles and attention to rectifying them without compromising future resident quality of care have become crucial to the success of Sunrise facilities.

Target Market Assessment. The ongoing success of any assisted living venture depends on the attention given to an appropriate target market assessment. In the case of Frederick, the experience gleaned by Sunrise over many years has a decided advantage. Important segments for analysis include the following:

- Standard **demographic reviews of potential clients** in existing tertiary markets (nursing homes, independent living for seniors, and other facilities providing personal care).
- Careful **attention to the forty-five- to sixty-five-year-olds,** whose parents move to reside close to them.
- **Reviews of the income of the forty-five- to sixty-five-year-olds** and of that of their parents, to determine ability to pay for private or semiprivate units.
- **Comparisons with the least expensive local nursing home** private-pay rates, determining whether they are greater than anticipated Sunrise semiprivate rates.

Recognizing that few seniors admit themselves to personal-care facilities prompted a change in assessment strategy away from traditional demographics only. A substantial proportion of future residents come from the group of parents who have moved to be closer to their children. Since the families of these seniors invariably admit them to care facilities, they must be one of the main groups for analysis in reviewing a potential market. Between 30 and 50 percent of future residents of Frederick and other Sunrise facilities are the parents of this group.

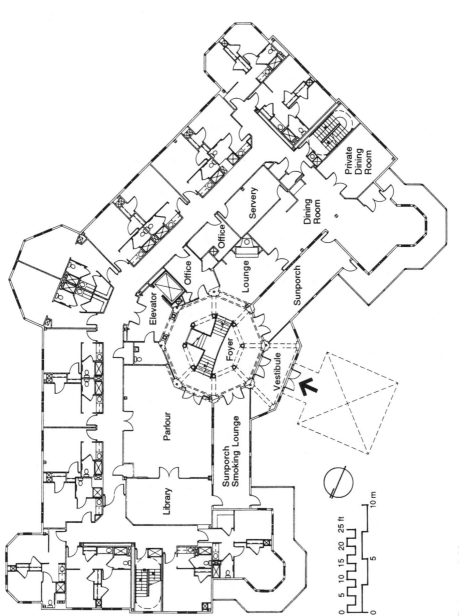

FIGURE 6.20. *First-floor plan*: A sun porch, dining room, parlor, library and lounge provide places for residents and family members to socialize.

As part of the assessment, it was hoped (but not certain) that the location of Frederick in a small town would improve opportunities to obtain a high-quality staff. In fact, this small, stable community has provided a core of career-oriented personnel committed to ensuring the quality of life of residents, many of whom have been family friends for years. This contrasts markedly with the transience expected of staff in a city setting.

Cost of Service. Able to benefit from established local resources and the expertise of Sunrise, Frederick aims to provide a very high quality of care to a predominantly middle- and upper-income elderly population. However, with conviction toward balancing social and investment objectives, Frederick also serves a 10 percent low-income-resident group. As a matter of social conscience, Sunrise is committed to supporting low-income residents. The innovative structure of service costs allows private-pay residents to subsidize the minority of low-income residents.

Base rates range from $25 to $110 daily, covering the majority of standard Activity of Daily Living (ADL) care needs. An extended-care package is also available for those whose needs require more intensive care, ranging from an additional $12.50 to $40 per day. These additional service costs generate only 5 to 8 percent of the total revenues, primarily because those who need extra care need very little, and approximately 74 percent need no extra care. Currently, only 15 percent pay the minimum charge of $12.50 for extended care, and only 5 percent pay more than $25, generally to meet their increased supervisory and medical needs during the last few weeks of life.

To accommodate residents of low or dwindling income, semiprivate units are charged at 60 percent of the private rate, significantly less than the industry standard of 75 percent, because Sunrise facilities typically maintain very high occupancy rates. This raises their break-even point; private competitors with lower occupancy rates must set their semiprivate rates at 75 to 80 percent of private charges to break even.

Lessons Learned with Potential for External Application

Fear of Luxury Creep. As new Sunrise buildings like Frederick are constructed or renovated, improvements based on experience should be expected to continue. Constant advancement toward improvement and the associated increase in facility attractiveness could easily go "over the edge," resulting in higher costs and reduced financial accessibility. In light of the goal to maintain a very user-friendly residential environment, this "luxury

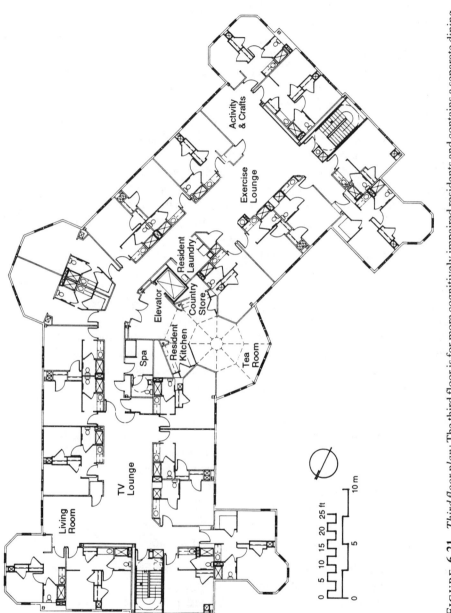

FIGURE 6.21. *Third floor plan:* The third floor is for more cognitively impaired residents and contains a separate dining room. Units are typically clustered around living rooms.

Living Room

TV Lounge

Spa

Resident Kitchen

Elevator

Resident Country Store

Laundry

Tea Room

Exercise Lounge

Activity & Crafts

0 5 10 15 20 25 ft

0 5 10 m

creep" could become a highly limiting factor if care is not taken to avoid overenhancing the Sunrise model. In actuality, of all possible problems this one is highly desirable.

Marketing Strategies. Facilities that carefully analyze local demographics and assess the potential resident population, including their families, often succeed. Facilities need to recognize the role administrators play in the community, as health care providers, and in resident and family acceptance of their service. Community networking before and during construction is an essential part of establishing a viable community presence. For this reason, the hiring of Sunrise administrators occurs during ground breaking. The subsequent educational process and growth in community trust, as health care providers and residents understand the Sunrise philosophy, build the referral network that will eventually maintain high occupancy rates without an expensive marketing program.

The Sunrise commitment to a 10 percent low-income residency has definite market value because it consolidates community trust. Once stable, Frederick, like other Sunrise facilities, has required no further advertising or marketing to stay full. Community service providers supply enough referrals to replace any residents that leave, both low-income and private-pay.

As the expected trend toward acquisitions continues and the construction of new buildings is limited to reduce start-up time, availability of trained administrators may become a concern.

Serving Residents with Special Needs. As is true in all Sunrise retirement homes, 45 percent of the residents at Frederick have discernible dementia problems, and 75 percent have limited dementia. The third floor of the building houses a special-needs program for those whose behavior is disruptive or bothersome. Residents with wandering behavior that compromises safety, disruptive dining behavior, conversation difficulties, and abusive or violent outbursts are handled with more supervision on a separate floor. As the level of care increases, the social advantages of having a separate floor also increase. Although the majority of residents are free to come and go, intermixing of all residents is highly encouraged. From a practical standpoint, dining areas remain separate, and from 7 P.M. until 9 P.M., third-floor residents are restricted to their floor.

This policy has allowed Frederick to keep residents with dementia in comfortable, quality surroundings long past what would have been typical had they not been separated. Rarely has a resident's behavior become so violent or verbally abusive that transfer to a nursing home was necessary.

Philosophically, it would be ideal to find a way to keep residents intermixed no matter what their dysfunction. From a practical, administrative, and financial standpoint, facilities like Frederick remain successful by providing specialized services in an environment tailored to the needs of residents.

At some point, behavioral and functional aberrations resulting from advanced dementia become disruptive and undermining to the residents and staff of assisted living facilities. It is to the credit of facilities like those represented in this case study chapter that every effort is made to accommodate increasing dysfunction, even if it necessitates some degree of separation.

Conclusions

In reflecting on lessons learned through reviewing the financing and management patterns of case study assisted living and those inspected during this survey, a number of important trends emerge.

1. Conventional or Innovative Financing

Diverse financing options for assisted living exist throughout the nation. However, as expected, most facilities appear to be financed through conventional means, primarily servicing a middle- to upper-income senior population. Financing innovations center around the use of mechanisms that encourage participation of lower-income frail elderly despite the negative impact of the 1986 Tax Reform Act that limited tax-exempt financing.

In general, our study demonstrates an urgent need for more creative public and private funding of assisted living for increasing numbers of low-income elderly. A major dent in providing service for them could be made if every facility exercised a social conscience and recruited 10 percent of its residents from low-income populations. It also suggests the need to encourage and advocate consistent and reliable third-party payment sources that increase less costly residential options for the frail low-income elderly.

2. Partnerships

Varying partnership structures appear to offer the greatest flexibility for meeting a variety of financing challenges. Risks can be spread and costs reduced most effectively through ventures that join multiple public and/or private parties with compatible areas of expertise. Such arrangements will only grow in importance if the shifting of the financial burden from the federal to state level continues. However, success of partnership arrangements is predicated on defining clear roles for all parties, based on a shared mission.

In the provision of service, partnerships that incorporate the assistance of residents, family members, and staff offer flexibility and increased opportunity for independence.

3. Institutional or Residential Model

Facilities reflecting an institutional environment can expect slow fill-up rates in the future. In the future, homelike assisted living settings will offer nursing home residents who do not need intensive medical care a viable alternative. At the very least, a savings of 25 percent can be expected in assisted living compared with nursing home care. Therefore better business opportunities should persist in the long-term care industry for facilities utilizing a homelike environment, especially if they effectively integrate cost-containing measures with a management philosophy promoting values of independence, dignity, individuality, and maximized functionality.

4. The Financing Process

Successful financing of assisted living facilities is an integrated process that begins with a comprehensive market assessment and proceeds with adequate planning, design, and marketing. This results in relatively quick fill-up rates and a stable residency. Projects recognized as having trouble financing ongoing operations appear to have either neglected or paid little attention to market assessment. Common problems include overbuilding, overestimating property value, overborrowing, depleting financial reserves, marketing poorly, inadequately screening potential residents, neglecting to include family members or health care providers in the marketing process, and mismanaging finances or operations.

5. Cost Reduction

Construction costs should not be reduced by cutting the quality of carpet, wallpapers, wall sconces, or moldings. These are the niceties that increase resident enjoyment of their home. Paul Klaassen of Sunrise Retirement Homes believes that the extra cost of these for each unit, amortized over thirty years, amounts to no more than fifty cents per day per resident. Better estimating of acceptable construction budgets in the beginning stages of the project can avoid the hassle of cutting corners later.

Challenges for the Future

1. The Regulatory Threat

One major future challenge is ensuring that developing regulations promote a homelike rather than an institutional setting for all frail and vulnerable elderly. The Medicaid Home and Community Care Options Act of 1990 provides limited funding for assisted living and acknowledges its value in long-term care. Industry advocates, developers, owners, and lenders must avoid any practices that promote regulation that reflects the traditional view of aging as a medical problem and therefore limits the opportunity for maximizing individuality, flexibility, and independence of residents.

2. Who Will Pay?

The domination of financing by conventional mechanisms that support private-pay middle- to upper-income frail elderly in assisted living can be expected to continue. However, as public entities recognize the potential for cost containment by serving low-income elderly in assisted living rather than nursing homes, public funding of assisted living should increase. In addition, we might expect that such organizations as Sunrise Retirement Homes, which is committed to serving and subsidizing a 10 percent low-income elderly resident mix, will continue to lead the way in providing service with a social conscience.

7. Design, Management, and Financing Directives

Factors That Influence Consumer Demand

The assisted living movement seems destined to revolutionize the way we think about long-term care. Chapter 1 introduced nine defining qualities and suggested twelve factors that have expedited interest in this developing alternative. The following four issues appear to be among the most powerful in directing consumer influences: demographics, preferences for a residential environment, cheaper and better alternatives, and inability of the nursing home to adapt.

Demographics

The number of people who will reach advanced age in the near future is extraordinary. Although many will want to stay in their own home, their increased frailty and a less substantial family support system will make it difficult for them to stay independent in the community. A growing number of frail people over the age of eighty-five will need protected environments, health care services, diagnostic/case management, and access to therapeutic activities like exercise to maintain their independence. Current projections from the U.S. Census Bureau and other reliable sources project that in the next fifty years we will have between four and seven times as many people over the age of eighty-five as we have currently. This means that the current 3.3 million people in this category may spiral upward to as much as

23.5 million (Guralnik, Yanagishita, and Schnieder 1988) by the year 2040. Rivlin and Weiner (1988) estimate that more than 60 percent of the current population over the age of eighty-five are disabled and that slightly more than 22 percent of this age group are currently in nursing homes.

Preferences for a Residential Environment

Those who need supportive services to maintain their independence will avoid nursing homes because they do not offer such basic considerations as privacy, autonomy, independence, control, and choice. The current older generation has had a role in institutionalizing their own parents in nursing home settings and are much more motivated to keep themselves out of an institution. Clearly, the system of long-term care as we know it has not been responsive to consumer interests and needs. Just as hospitals have become more competitive in the last five years, long-term care will be forced to adapt in ways that are consistent with consumer demands.

Some policymakers believe that the Health Care Financing Agency (HCFA), which is charged with containing health care costs, has been reluctant to advocate improvements to the current long-term-care system. One reason is that making the system more responsive to consumer desires might make it more popular and thus more costly to the government, which pays the majority of the costs through Medicare/Medicaid. There appears to be a financial incentive for keeping the nursing home threatening and undesirable.

Cheaper and Better Alternatives

Generally, in unregulated sectors of the economy when a less expensive but better-quality alternative is introduced, it captures market segment. The highly regulated nursing home sector has matured in ways that are inconsistent with consumer demand, and it is unattractively priced. Assisted living represents a viable alternative because it is sensitive to consumer demands and is less expensive.

If you examine other care delivery systems elsewhere (e.g., northern Europe), you find more home care services delivered within a residential environment. Looking at the European system as a marker for comparison, we could probably place 40 percent of current nursing home residents in residential environments with more case-managed personal and health care services. Experiments like the Oregon assisted living program have shown

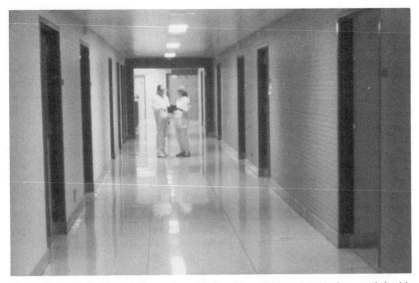

FIGURE 7.1. *A nursing home is typically planned like a hospital around double loaded corridors:* The lack of detail, the wide corridors, and the glare from light fixtures and reflection from the floor give it an institutional look.

how nursing home beds can be reduced and overall health care costs on a per capita basis can be contained (Lewin–ICF 1992; Kane and Wilson 1993).

Inability of the Nursing Home to Adapt

The nursing home, tied to a set of rigid regulations, which are not responsive to consumers or to providers, seems destined to fail. Like any protected industry, it has been allowed to grow in directions that are inconsistent with consumer interests. Again, a look at European models clearly demonstrates what has been sacrificed. Therapeutic models in Europe use smaller clusters of units that are more integrated with community services. Many use therapeutic activities as the basis for building competency. Finally, buildings are not required to meet distorted safety requirements. Our system of litigation, which has sought to police the industry, has also made it impossible to test out new ideas. As with anything else that has reached the end of its functional purpose, the nursing home must change or be replaced. The current situation combines narrow-minded regulation, litigable risk, and a stingy system of reimbursement in an industry that has settled for a less than perfect alter-

native. For all these reasons, long-term care will likely not continue as we
have known it.

Assisted Living Directives

What changes are necessary? What will this new model of care be like?
How will it develop? What will characterize it as different from current
long-term-care choices? These questions have been the basis of this work.
The following twenty directives summarize the major points in the preceding six chapters. The format utilized states important principles and then
backs them with a rationale and implications that could be drawn from a
design and management perspective. The twenty directives are separated
into four categories based on how they appear to influence the development
of the building concept, the physical design of the environment, the care
and management philosophy, and the financing of this alternative.

These categories attempt to provide a system of organization. However,
the boundaries between them are fluid, and arguments could be made to
reshuffle them under the same or a different system of categorization. It is
hoped that they will provide a useful summary and a way of examining how
we can define assisted living as a new care philosophy and building typology.

Concept Development
One: Defining assisted living
Two: Privacy, autonomy, and independence
Three: Choice and control
Four: Therapeutic vs. prosthetic environment
Five: Medical vs. residential models
Six: Aging in place
Seven: Community integration
Physical Environment
Eight: Complete dwelling unit design
Nine: Sensory stimulation
Ten: Indoor/outdoor connections
Eleven: Functionally and behaviorally responsive rooms
Twelve: Regulations and oversight
Care Management
Thirteen: Decentralized management and decision making
Fourteen: Family, staff, and resident relationships
Fifteen: Uniquely prescribed services

One: Defining Assisted Living

Assisted living is a residential long-term-care alternative that involves the managed delivery of uniquely prescribed health and personal-care services within a residential environment.

This is important because

1. Traditional nursing homes are designed, managed, and operated as institutions.
2. The residential character of the setting allows residents and staff to feel as if they are operating in a housing environment rather than a health care institution.
3. Personalized, managed care that involves the participation of residents and their families builds competency and encourages autonomy.

Management and design implications

A. Smaller-scale settings of sixty units or less are perceived as less overwhelming to residents.
B. Personalized assistance should be based on a therapeutic model of intervention that takes into consideration the preferences, needs, and desires of residents in a way that encourages independence.
C. Dwelling units should be private and large enough to support a life-style that promotes a sense of independence and autonomy.

Two: Privacy, Autonomy, and Independence

Unit design and management philosophy should accommodate privacy, encourage autonomy, and reward independence.

This is important because

1. Exercising independence is a basic human need that is highly related to feelings of self-worth.

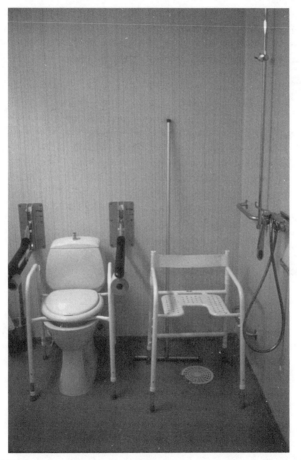

FIGURE 7.2. *European bathrooms often specify a tile floor with hand held fixtures and drainage in one corner:* This maximizes space in the bathroom for toileting transfers and assistance with bathing.

2. Autonomy can be encouraged through the specification of a complete private dwelling unit.
3. Environments that do not provide the necessary options to exercise independence often encourage dependence.
4. Most nursing home accommodations are double-occupancy units.

Management and design implications

A. Placing locks on dwelling unit doors is a simple enhancement with profound overtones. Lockable doors give residents the option of exercising control. Staff members also sense the need for privacy and territoriality and knock before entering.
B. Dwelling unit designs with kitchenettes and private bathrooms encourage independent decision making and support a diversity of human needs and competencies.
C. Designing the housing arrangement so that it allows residents to easily view and experience outdoor patios and courtyards increases their sense of freedom.

Three: Choice and Control

Dwelling units, common spaces, and supportive services should be designed to offer maximum personal control and optimum choice.

This is important because

1. Choice and control have been found to be important psychosocial variables that affect resident satisfaction.
2. The essence of institutionalization usually involves narrowing options and choices as well as controlling behaviors and access.

Management and design implications

A. Choice can be offered even to severely cognitively impaired residents through such techniques as allowing them to select the entree they want by visually inspecting choices.
B. Allowing residents to "preview" spaces by seeing into them before they enter adds predictability and control.
C. Resident food-tasting panels provide another way to channel dissatisfaction with meal services through constructive criticism.
D. Decentralized management approaches often allow residents to exercise more effective decision making.
E. Choice and control add complexity to an environment but can be confusing or frustrating for some residents. The residents' desire for choice should be balanced against their ability to exercise it.
F. Enhancing self-mastery encourages other independent behaviors.

Four: Therapeutic vs. Prosthetic Environment

The environment should be designed not only to support but to stimulate therapeutic outcomes.

This is important because

1. A prosthetic environment by definition provides enough support to overcome a loss in ability. A therapeutic environment assumes

FIGURE 7.3. *Sliding pocket or barn doors to bedrooms or bathrooms are typically employed in European housing for the frail:* Eliminating the swing of the door makes it easier to manipulate within tight rooms.

the older person will be challenged slightly beyond his or her current capacity in order to build new strengths.

2. The idea of a therapeutic environment can form the basis of a powerful and pervasive management and care-giving culture, which seeks to encourage independence.

Management and design implications

A. Therapy should be defined broadly to include such activities as maintaining oneself, helping with the laundry, socializing with other residents, and taking part in a routine exercise regimen.

B. Safety considerations should be balanced against ways of increasing stimulation. This will allow residents to maintain motivation while they develop new abilities.

C. Therapeutic activities should be conveniently located, frequently available, and psychologically inviting.

D. A care philosophy that challenges residents to do as much as they can for themselves results in positive feelings of self-esteem and a greater sense of independence.

Five: Medical vs. Residential Models

Assisted living should be conceptualized as housing with services rather than as a model of institutional medical care.

This is important because

1. Older residents prefer a residential environment in which services are available as needed to the conventional institutional setting.
2. Housing environments are generally less expensive to build, maintain, and operate than conventional institutions. Project costs can thus be lower.
3. A residential context provides continuity with past living arrangements and a greater degree of personal freedom.

Management and design implications

A. Medical models of assisted living are often designed to be remodeled in the future for skilled nursing. The only difference between skilled care and some personal care models is that rooms are single occupied and carpeted.
B. Medical models often incorporate care-giving philosophies consistent with the culture of a nursing home. The outcome can be a setting where individual autonomy, privacy, and dignity are valued less than they should be.

Six: Aging in Place

The environment and the services available should be organized to maintain residents as long as possible in the same dwelling unit.

This is important because

1. Moving residents from one place to another can be disorienting. If it signals a permanent move to an institutional setting, it can be depressing.

FIGURE 7.4. *Programming should seek to recognize the uniqueness of each resident:* A range of activities should be encouraged.

2. Most residents prefer to stay in the same environment and increase the level of service they receive.

3. The new portable equipment and advanced communications technology available today make it easier to provide home nursing assistance in a residential environment.

Management and design implications

A. Units should be sized for handicapped accessibility as well as assistance in bathing and toileting.

B. Services should be designed to be increased when the need for more intensive support is required.

C. Ways of responding to changing needs and abilities should be considered in the design. For example, a larger handicapped-accessible bathroom can be designed with storage cabinets, grab bars, and other detachable aids that fill in the room to create a more intimate space that the ambulatory person can use for support while walking. These cabinets and bars should be easily removed when more circulation space for a walker or wheelchair is needed.

D. The concept of the Continuing Care Retirement Community (CCRC) is based on residents physically moving to differing types of housing and service arrangements when their abilities decline and they need more assistance. This concept has been encouraged by building codes, licensing requirements, and assumptions about service delivery efficiency. Greater emphasis should be placed on keeping residents in one place and adding services.

Seven: Community Integration

The housing development should seek to fit into the surrounding context complementing the neighborhood and appearing as a normal addition to the housing stock.

FIGURE 7.5. *Nurse's stations in European nursing homes are often attractive approachable alcove spaces:* Residents can sit on a chair or roll their wheelchair up to the table to discuss a problem.

This is important because

1. Institutions–because of zoning requirements, building codes, and assumptions about character–often look quite different from the surrounding housing stock.
2. Many facilities attempt to provide all services within a self-contained model. This isolates the housing from a normal inter-dependent relationship with neighborhood stores and services. It also reduces choice and promotes a narrow view of life within the housing environment.
3. Facilities often do not provide services or activities for people who live in the surrounding neighborhood. This can further isolate residents from older and younger people living outside the building.

Management and design implications

A. Encouraging residents to continue personal business relation-ships with shops and services in their old neighborhood can link them with another familiar context.
B. Providing special services to neighborhood residents makes the housing appear community centered rather than self-contained. This doesn't necessarily mean buildings must provide clinical services to the neighborhood. Mixed-use retail shops that sell flowers or ice cream can serve the neighborhood as well as residents, making the housing more approachable and community related.
C. Inviting other age groups, like preschoolers, in for craft activities or specific events creates relationships that are emotionally satisfying and intellectually stimulating.
D. Providing home-delivered services to neighborhood residents such as meals on wheels or home help services makes the housing an important neighborhood resource.

Eight: Complete Dwelling Unit Design

Assisted living dwelling units should be large enough to accommodate a full bathroom, a kitchenette, and a guest for an overnight stay.

This is important because

1. A full bathroom provides the option of preserving privacy by taking an assisted shower within the dwelling unit and avoiding complete dependence on a central tub or shower room.
2. The option of preparing food in the dwelling unit adds to the repertoire of independent behaviors available to residents.
3. Children, grandchildren, friends, or private care givers who want to spend the night need room to sleep.

Management and design implications

A. Dwelling units larger than 250 square feet are necessary to fit these requirements.
B. Food preparation and storage space need not be large and sophisticated. The kitchenette offers symbolic choice as well as instrumental value.
C. A single burner for limited cooking can be designed with a timer switch that safeguards its use for residents with memory loss.
D. Bathrooms should be large enough to accommodate an assistant who may help in bathing or transferring residents to the toilet. However, the room should also be designed for the ambulatory resident who needs to hold onto fixtures, knobs, and surfaces to steady herself.
E. Treating the dwelling unit as a complete residential environment gives the family and friends of the resident the sense she is living independently, rather than in an institution.
F. Zoning and regulatory requirements can limit kitchen facilities in each unit. Board-and-care and/or personal-care licensure refer to beds rather than dwelling units in their nomenclature. Thus regulations based on an inappropriate narrow definition of this housing type may preclude the use of kitchen facilities.

Nine: Sensory Stimulation

The environment should pleasantly stimulate the senses of hearing, smelling, tasting, seeing, and feeling.

This is important because

1. The normal aging process leads to decreases in sensory ability. This means that stronger sensory input may be necessary.

FIGURE 7.6. *Three dimensional graphics help blind or visually impaired residents identify rooms:* This project in Denmark uses cast ceramic plates to code residential wings.

2. Institutional environments often offend the senses. This can include uncontrolled noises that are poorly mitigated and smells that are noxious and disturbing.

Management and design implications

A. Positive sensory inputs can include soothing music, large-scale readable graphics, pleasant scents that stimulate positive memories, delicious food, and wall surfaces, furniture, and accessories that introduce different textures.
B. The environment should be designed to eliminate noxious and disturbing noises, especially while residents are asleep or resting.
C. For the blind and the deaf, multiple cuing devices and Braille lettering are necessary.
D. Sensory stimulation can also involve observing activities, social interaction, and intellectually challenging group discussions.

Ten: Indoor/Outdoor Connections

Physical, visual, and psychological access should be provided to outdoor areas that are located adjacent to interior spaces.

This is important because

1. Outdoor areas located near interior common spaces can support social activities or be used passively to watch outdoor activities.

FIGURE 7.7. *Nursing homes in Denmark almost always have outdoor patios adjacent to units where residents and family members can socialize:* The majority of nursing home units are single occupied and many have small kitchenettes.

2. Residents with ambulatory difficulties often limit their use of the surrounding neighborhood. This constriction of home range makes convenient access to gardens and patios more important.
3. Outdoor areas provide a unique setting for plant materials, birds, butterflies, small mammals, natural sunlight, and gentle wind currents. This can add variety and stimulation.
4. Off-site views of neighborhood activities provide a "window to the world" that is stimulating and interest provoking.

Management and design implications

A. Outdoor garden and patio spaces should extend popular interior common spaces by enticing residents to go outside.
B. Porch, arcade, and balcony spaces that are protected but open to the elements are popular places to visit, particularly when they provide views of the surrounding neighborhood.
C. Greenhouse windows, bay windows, and window seats are protected interior spaces that are thrust into the landscape. Their configuration can make exterior landscapes more visible.
D. Management can encourage outdoor space use by organizing events such as picnics and barbecues.
E. Ground cover, flowers, herbs, and vertically trained plants offer attractive controlled views.

Eleven: Functionally and Behaviorally Responsive Rooms

Common spaces, corridors, and entry lobbies should support a range of special activities and behaviors that are of therapeutic benefit to residents.

This is important because

1. When spaces are not designed to support specific use patterns or therapeutic ideas, they rarely benefit residents in a creative and productive way.
2. The perceived life-style of a setting is often based on the organization and availability of activities. The environment should support a range of options and choices. The design of interior and exterior rooms can prompt use patterns or appear vague and lifeless.
3. The activity level of a setting is often affected by the location, design, and relationship of common spaces. The arrangement of these spaces can determine whether a building is experienced as friendly or alienating.

Management and design implications

A. Rehearsing possible activity patterns and room uses helps to test their viability and fit.
B. Some rooms, such as a hospitality lounge or country kitchen, must be accessible from a nearby circulation corridor to stimulate spontaneous social activity.
C. Other spaces, such as a barber/beauty shop, auditorium, or clinic, operate by appointment or involve planned events. In these settings, spontaneous use is minimal.
D. Still other spaces, such as a card room, crafts room, or exercise area, should be private enough to assure comfort but visible enough to stimulate residents to become involved.

Twelve: Regulations and Oversight

Regulations should establish a standard for service quality that is performance based and flexible enough to accommodate creative experimentation.

This is important because

1. Nursing home regulations are frequently rigid in terms of both environment and staffing. This leads to narrow, inflexible appli-

FIGURE 7.8. *The most popular places to sit are places where residents have a view of activities:* This Finnish service house has a number of sitting areas that operate as "perches" surrounding a large landscaped atrium.

cations that are insensitive to therapeutic needs and may inadvertently encourage dependence.

2. To date, assisted living has escaped narrowly framed regulations. This has been generally positive, providing further evidence that regulations, as they are currently conceived, stifle creative and progressive thinking about care giving.

Management and design implications

A. Regulations that keep residents from "working" within the setting make it impossible to pursue therapies that involve such activities of daily living as shopping, cleaning, food preparation, and laundry.

B. Nursing home regulations that limit the distance from the nurses' station to resident rooms encourage geometric (i.e., X, T, Y), double-loaded corridor configurations and require a high percentage of two-bed rooms. These shapes are typical of such highly controlled institutions as hospitals and prisons.

C. Regulations should be specific enough to communicate intention but flexible enough to encourage experimentation.

D. Codes and regulations that are contradictory, narrow choices and confuse options in institutions and housing environments.

E. Regulatory exceptions and trade-offs should be structured to encourage more experimental models to be tested and evaluated.

Thirteen: Decentralized Management and Decision Making

Decentralizing responsibility so that the staff works with resident groups of ten to fifteen people allows individuality and creativity to flourish.

This is important because

1. Care givers working with smaller resident groups can develop a unique operating philosophy that reflects the personalities of residents and staff. Allowing these group identities to emerge promotes individuality and diversity.
2. Care-giving approaches can be custom fit, facilitating more effective individual communication and building stronger group identities.
3. Physical environments that are "typical" in footprint configuration can look very different when they are decorated or remodeled in specific ways that represent the care-giving philosophy of smaller subdivided units.
4. The most influential and thought-provoking interventions can come from expressing individual identity, diversity, and communality.

Management and design implications

A. Decentralization allows policy-making to be localized. Residents can influence meal service, specify activities, and aid in the evaluation and recruitment of new staff members.
B. Decentralization allows one group to eat together family style with staff members, another group to take meals around small tables in restaurant style, and a third group to take most meals by themselves in their own rooms. A highly decentralized management philosophy encourages diversity.
C. The decoration and layout of common spaces can also reflect resident preferences and influences by including furniture and accessories loaned by residents. Changes in the furnishing or organization of spaces can also reflect specific ideas about the group personality of each resident cluster.

Fourteen: Family, Staff, and Resident Relationships

The operating culture of the organization should strive to integrate the efforts of family members with staff professionals and to stimulate informal helping exchanges between residents.

This is important because

1. Family members can stimulate recall and focus residents' interest on a range of emotional and historical topics.
2. Staff members can learn valuable and informative insights from family members about the interests, preferences, and habits of residents. These can lead to more animated, engaging, and personal discussions with staff.
3. Partnerships between paid professional care givers and family members and friends can informalize care giving. This increases family participation and makes help appear more natural and less clinical.

FIGURE 7.9. *A day care program for memory impaired older people can be offered to residents as well as people living in the surrounding neighborhood:* In this project both constituencies are well served.

Management and design implications

   A. Family members can build relationships with residents through such instrumental tasks as doing the laundry, working in the garden, tidying up the unit, or having lunch together. This can give a family visit both focus and meaning.

   B. Family members can inform staff about topics that engage residents in meaningful conversations about specific interests (e.g., gardening, pets, past experiences, family, work activities, and travel).

   C. Resident and family involvement in supervising self-care activities can encourage autonomy and independence.

   D. Regulations often limit the participation of family members and friends in instrumental activities, thus discouraging the proliferation of different types of informal/formal care-giver partnerships.

Fifteen: Uniquely Prescribed Services

The housing should provide a unique and flexible service package for each resident.

This is important because

1. It encourages older residents to exercise control over aspects of their life they have the ability to manage.
2. It minimizes expenses by challenging older residents to do as much as they can for themselves.
3. It encourages an attitude of diversity that recognizes the differential abilities, specific interests, and changing needs of each resident.
4. It can involve families in providing meaningful care and assistance that compliments staff and resident efforts.

Management and design implications

A. Case assessments conducted on a monthly basis allow staff to review needed services by monitoring general health status and evaluating past efforts.
B. Dwelling unit fixtures, HVAC controls, windows, doors, and cabinet work should be designed to compensate for declining muscle strength and manipulation ability, thus facilitating aging in place.

Sixteen: Risk Management

Freedom, choice, flexibility, and control should correspond to a resident's capability to exercise independent behaviors safely.

This is important because

1. Regulations have traditionally established rigid requirements for safety that limit freedom. Many older people and their families find this paternalistic and counterproductive.
2. Risk taking is an important aspect of preserving dignity.
3. Too much choice and freedom can create uncertainty and risk for which there is little psychological reward.

Management and design implications

A. Case management approaches that identify individual resident interests, values, habits, behaviors, and desires can be the basis for establishing a unique program of care.
B. Family members, older residents, neighboring residents, and paid professionals can be involved in care partnerships that benefit everyone.
C. Outfitting a dwelling unit with a kitchen and a food preparation space provides options and choices for aging in place and an environment that can challenge residents as their competency declines.
D. Some activities, like smoking and eating unhealthy foods, exacerbate diseases and deleterious conditions. These impacts should be clearly identified and explained to residents, but the essence of choice is allowing residents to exercise behaviors that are important to them and not just optimizing healthy behaviors over all other considerations.
E. Risk management must also take into consideration the safety of other residents and how their welfare can be affected negatively.

Seventeen: Caring for the Physically and Mentally Frail

Assisted living attracts both mentally and physically frail older people, who can require different support services and care-giving strategies.

This is important because

1. The integration or segregation of these populations can have a major effect on how management and care giving are organized and on the identity of the setting.
2. Neither the integration nor the segregation of the mentally frail has emerged as a preferable approach.
3. The mentally frail can disturb other residents because of behavioral outbursts that range from the annoying to the threatening.

Management and design implications

A. Three general models are most common: (1) an integrated mainstreaming of both populations, (2) segregation of the severely

FIGURE 7.10. *Sunrise uses a Victorian style building that appears residential and approachable:* Porches, bay window turrets, a low eve height and residential detailing give the building a friendly look.

impaired in a separate area of an integrated setting, and (3) a segregated building that houses only the mentally impaired.

B. Approximately 40 percent of the older residents in assisted living facilities visited for this study experienced memory loss
problems.

C. Complete integration of all populations is conceptually the most
desirable approach, but it is fraught with problems that limit its
applicability and complicate management.

D. In northern Europe, the Swedes and Danes have chosen to pursue different approaches to the problem. The Danes have mainstreamed populations throughout service houses. The Swedes
have chosen to serve the mentally frail in small, decentralized
group homes.

E. The specific behavioral problems of Alzheimer's residents, such
as wandering and rummaging, make integrated settings difficult
to manage. When residents reach a stage where behaviors affect
others, they are frequently forced to move to a nursing home.

F. Separate facilities work well, but economy-of-scale considerations often require that their size be large and frequently overwhelming.

G. Separate floors or sections of an integrated building allow victims in early stages to be mainstreamed throughout the building.
When they reach a point where focused attention is necessary,
they can be moved. Placing dementia residents in one area allows staff training and therapeutic programs to be more efficient
and effective.

Eighteen: Maintaining and Training Staff

The success of any facility is based on the ability of staff members to implement a sensitive, humane philosophy of care.

This is important because

1. Staff members provide the glue that links residents, families, and friends to the housing environment. Their attitude, approach, and philosophy shape the life-style of the setting.
2. The attitudes of staff members toward their job, the residents, and their visitors have enormous impact on the lives of residents.
3. Staff members who assume behaviors consistent with the culture of a nursing home can cause damage and alienation in assisted living. Staff members must be trained to recognize how care giving differs in this context.

Management and design implications

A. Well-trained staff members preserve and enhance the privacy of residents and challenge their competency by involving them in appropriate self-care activities.

FIGURE 7.11. *Courtyard spaces are popular in assisted living projects:* They allow outdoor spaces to be easily defined and activities contained on small sites.

B. Assigning staff to care for the needs of a group of residents allows the staff to build strong, effective, and congenial caregiving relationships that are more satisfying to the staff and less confusing to the resident.

C. Staff members must be motivated by training that raises their consciousness and by a corporate culture that rewards their observations and creativity in providing care. Decentralized authority and responsibility aid this operating philosophy.

Nineteen: Reducing the Cost Burden

The increasing cost of care is likely to be most affected by reductions in the cost of building construction and reductions in the amount of formal care provided, which is augmented by self-care support and family assistance.

This is important because

1. The current high cost of institutionalization quickly reduces the life savings of private-pay nursing home patients.
2. Sharing responsibility for important tasks with family members and getting the older person to do as much as possible can reduce the amount of support needed.

Management and design implications

A. Building codes, regulatory requirements, and legal ambiguities make it difficult for assisted living arrangements to create partnerships with family members that can reduce costs.
B. Building code requirements for institutional occupancies often drive up the cost of construction.
C. Services mandated through licensure may not be necessary when assessed on a case-by-case basis. In fact, too many services may encourage learned helplessness.
D. Assisted living settings that can give the same level of service as some patients receive in a nursing home can generally provide a larger, more private dwelling unit at a cost that is 25 to 30 percent less than that of a nursing home.
E. Even though approaches can be developed that optimize cost considerations, the cost of caring for an increasing number of old frail people in the next forty years will be enormous.

Twenty: Developing Subsidizing Mechanisms

As a society, we must put into place reimbursement mechanisms and housing finance programs that encourage the development of assisted living housing in place of nursing homes.

This is important because

1. Few federal reimbursement programs or housing finance programs support this type of housing.
2. Massive investment in this housing/service combination will be necessary to create enough stock to equal the demand.

Management and design implications

A. Retrofitting existing nursing homes, hospitals, and other care settings will involve careful thinking and a reorganization of the way care is delivered.
B. Standards developed for federal or state reimbursement for assisted living may cause rigidity around a few existing models of assisted living. Flexibility and innovation should continue to be high priorities as our knowledge of new care-giving approaches develops and is better understood.
C. Low-income people without functioning family supports also need to be supported in these settings.
D. Mechanisms that involve broad-based partnerships between community agencies and private providers spread development risk and take advantage of a wide range of experience.
E. Using private-pay residents to subsidize a small percentage (10 percent) of low-income residents allows developments targeted toward middle- to higher-income residents to contribute to this problem.

References

Adam, E. A. 1993. *The Feasibility of Converting Resident Care Facilities Into Assisted Living Facilities.* Master in City Planning thesis, Boston: MIT.

AIA Foundation. 1985. *Design for Aging: An Architect's Guide.* Washington, D.C.: AIA Press.

ALFAA. 1990. "The Medicaid Home and Community Care Options Act." Unpublished paper.

American Association of Homes for the Aging. 1992. *AAHA Assisted Living State Code Workbook: State-by-State Physical Plant Requirements and Contacts.* Washington, D.C.: AARP.

American Association of Retired Persons and Stein Gerontological Institute. 1993. *Life-Span Design of Residential Environments for an Aging Population.* Washington, D.C.: AARP.

American Institute of Architects. 1992. *Design for Aging: 1992 Review.* Washington, D.C.: The Institute.

Benjamin, A. and R. Newcomer. 1986. "Board and Care Housing: An Analysis of State Differences." *Research on Aging* 8(3).

Blatter, A. and E. Marty-Nelson. 1989. "An Overview of the Low-Income Housing Tax Credit." In Mark S. Dennison, ed., *Zoning and Planning Law Handbook.* New York: Clark, Boardman.

Bowe, J. 1990. "Inspiring Independence and Autonomy." *Contemporary Long Term Care* (October):48–50.

Calkins, M. 1988. *Designing for Dementia: Planning Environments for the Elderly and Confused.* Owings Mills, Md. National Health Publishing.

Carstens, D. Y. 1990. "Housing and Outdoor Spaces for the Elderly," in C. Marcus and C. Francis, eds., *People Places: Design Guidelines for Urban Open Space.* New York: Van Nostrand Reinhold.

Cohen, U. and G. Weisman. 1991. *Holding on to Home: Designing Environments for People with Dementia*. Baltimore: Johns Hopkins University Press.

Cohen, U. and K. Day. 1991. *Contemporary Environments for People with Dementia*. Milwaukee: Center for Architecture and Urban Planning Research, University of Wisconsin–Milwaukee.

Cohen, U., G. Weisman, K. Ray, V. Steiner, J. Rand, and R. Toye. 1988. *Environments for People with Dementia: Design Guide*. Milwaukee: Center for Architecture and Urban Planning Research, University of Wisconsin–Milwaukee.

Connerly, E. 1990. "Housing Trust Funds: New Resources for Low-Income Housing." *Journal of Housing* 47(2).

Council of State Housing Agencies & National Association of State Units on Aging. 1987. "Effects of the 1986 Tax Act on Financing of Housing for the Elderly." Washington, D.C.: Council of State Housing Agencies and NASUA.

de Reus, M. 1987. *Serving the Elderly: Securing Financing*. Report published for Backen Arrigoni & Ross, San Francisco.

Dobkin, L. 1989. *The Board and Care System: A Regulatory Jungle*. Washington, D.C.: Consumer Affairs Program, AARP.

Green, I., B. Fedewa, C. Johnston, W. Jackson, and H. Deardorff. 1975. *Housing for the Elderly: The Development and the Design Process*. New York: Van Nostrand Reinhold.

Green, L. 1990. "Humor and Lighthearted Activities." In D. Coons, ed., *Specialized Dementia Care Units*. Baltimore: Johns Hopkins University Press, pp. 175–188.

Guggenheim, J. 1988a. "Using Tax Credits: Financing Rehabilitation." *Journal of Housing* 45(4).

Guggenheim, J. 1988b. "Alternate Financing." *Journal of Housing* 45(4).

Guralnik, J., M. Yanagishta, and E. Schneider. 1988. "Projecting the Older Population of the United States: Lessons from the Past and Prospects for the Future." *The Milbank Quarterly* 66(2):283–308.

Hawes, C., J. Wildfire, and L. Lux (1993a). *The Regulation of Board and Care Homes: Results of a Survey in the 50 States and the District of Columbia—National Summary*. Washington, D.C.: AARP.

Hawes, C., J. Wildfire, and L. Lux (1993b). *The Regulation of Board and Care Homes: Results of a Survey in the 50 States and the District of Columbia—State Summaries*. Washington, D.C.: AARP.

Heumann, L. and D. Boldy. 1982. *Housing for the Elderly: Policy Formulation in Europe and North America*. London: St. Martin's Press.

Hiatt, L. 1991. *Nursing Home Renovation Designed for Reform*. Boston: Butterworth Architecture.

Hoglund, D. 1985. *Housing for the Elderly: Privacy and Independence in Environments for the Aging*. New York: Van Nostrand Reinhold.

Howell, S. 1980. *Designing for Aging: Patterns of Use*. Cambridge: MIT Press.

Jarvis, J. 1989. "Seniors Counsel Wayward Teens." *Senior World of Orange County* 5(11):1, 18.

Jenkins, R.C. 1992. *Developing Assisted Living Facilities: The Impact of State Licensing*. Master of Science in Real Estate Development thesis, Boston: MIT.

Kalymun, M. 1990. "Toward a Definition of Assisted-Living." In L. Pastalan, ed., *Optimizing Housing for the Elderly: Homes Not Houses*. New York: Hayworth Press, pp. 97–132.

Kane, R. and K. B. Wilson. 1993. *Assisted Living in the United States: A New Paradigm for Residential Care for Frail Older Persons*. Washington, D. C.: AARP.

Kane, R., L. Illuston, R. Kane, and J. Nyman. 1990. *Meshing Services with Housing: Lessons from Adult Foster Care and Assisted Living in Oregon*. Minneapolis: Long-Term Care DECISIONS Resource Center, University of Minnesota.

Laventhol & Horwath. 1989. *Retirement Housing Industry, 1988*. Philadelphia: Laventhol & Horwath.

Lawton, M. P. 1975. *Planning and Managing Housing for the Elderly*. New York: Wiley.

Lewin-ICF. 1992. *Policy Synthesis on Assisted Living for the Frail Elderly*. Report prepared for the Assistant Secretary of Planning and Evaluation, DHHS, November.

Long Term Care National Resource Center at UCLA/USC. 1989. *Assisted Living Resource Guide*. Los Angeles: The Long Term Care National Resource Center at UCLA/USC.

Malkin, J. 1992. *Hospital Interior Architecture: Creating Healing Environments for Special Patient Populations*. New York: Van Nostrand Reinhold.

McCarthy, M. 1992. "Older People Will Do Anything to Avoid Life in Nursing Home." *Wall Street Journal,* December 3, pp. A1, A6.

Mollica, R., R. Ladd, S. Dietsche, K. Wilson, and B. Ryther. 1992. *Building Assisted Living for the Elderly into Public Long Term Care Policy: A Technical Guide for States*. Waltham, Mass.: The Center for Vulnerable Populations, The National Academy for State Health Policy, and the Institute for Health Policy, Brandeis University.

Morgan, M. H. 1960. *Vitruvius: The Ten Books of Architecture*. New York: Dover.

Morton, D. 1981. "Congregate Living." *Progressive Architecture* 62(8):64–68.

Mullen, A. J. 1989. "Nationwide Absorption Rates: The Critical Element in the Feasibility of Senior Living Projects." Unpublished paper.

Mullen, A. J. 1991. "The Assisted Living Industry: An Assessment." *Retirement Housing Report,* January.

National Association of Home Builders. 1987. *Senior Housing: A Development and Management Handbook*. Washington ,D.C.: National Association of Home Builders of the United States.

Nenno, M. and G. Colyer. 1989. "Trust Funds: New Trends in Housing and Finance." *Journal of Housing* 46(1).

Newcomer, R., S. Roderick, and S. Preston. 1992. "Assisted Living and Nursing Unit Use Among Continuing Care Retirement Community Residents." Paper presented at the Annual Meeting of the American Association of Homes for the Aging (AAHA), Boston.

Pynoos, J. 1990. "Public Policy and Aging in Place—Identifying the Problems and Potential Solutions." In David Tilson, ed., *Aging in Place: Supporting the Frail Elderly in Residential Environment*. Glenview, Ill.: Scott, Foresman, pp. 167–208.

Regnier, V. 1985. *Behavioral and Environmental Aspects of Outdoor Space Use in*

Housing for the Elderly. Los Angeles: School of Architecture, Andrus Gerontology Center, University of Southern California.

Regnier, V. 1992. "European Models of Assisted Living Housing for Mentally and Physically Frail Older People." (Videotape.) Los Angeles: National Eldercare Institute on Housing and Supportive Services, University of Southern California.

Regnier, V. 1994. *Assisted Living Housing for the Elderly: Design Innovations from the United States and Europe.* New York: Van Nostrand Reinhold.

Regnier, V. and J. Pynoos. 1987. *Housing of the Aged: Design Directives and Policy Considerations.* New York: Elsevier.

Regnier, V. and J. Pynoos. 1992. "Environmental Interventions for Cognitively Impaired Older Persons." In J. Birren, B. Sloane, and G. Cohen, eds., *Handbook of Mental Health and Aging,* Second Edition. New York: Academic Press, pp. 763–792.

Regnier, V., D. Hoglund, and P. Klaassen. 1993. "1993 Architectural Design Awards." *Contemporary Long Term Care* 16 (6): 41–60.

Regnier, V. 1993. "Innovative Concepts in Assisted Housing." *Ageing International.*

Regnier, V., J. Hamilton, and S. Yatabe. 1991. *Best Practices in Assisted Living: Innovations in Design, Management and Financing.* Los Angeles: National Eldercare Institute on Housing and Supportive Services, University of Southern California.

Rivlin, A. and J. Wiener. 1988. *Caring for the Disabled Elderly.* Washington D.C.: The Brookings Institute.

Seip, D. 1989a. "First National Assisted Living Industry Survey." *Contemporary Long Term Care* 12(70): 69–70.

Seip, D. 1989b. "Free-Standing Assisted Living Trends." *Contemporary Long Term Care* 12(12):20, 22–23.

Seip, D. 1989c. "Tallying the First National Assisted Living Survey." *Contemporary Long Term Care* 12(10):28, 30, 32–33.

Seip, D. 1990. *The Survival Handbook for Developers of Assisted Living.* Boca Raton, Fla.: The Seip Group.

Special Committee on Aging. 1989. *Aging America: Trends and Projections Series 101E.* Washington, D.C.: U.S. Government Printing Office.

Stegman, M. 1986. *Housing Finance & Public Policy.* New York: Van Nostrand Reinhold.

Struyk, R., D. Page, S. Newman, M. Carroll, M. Ueno, B. Cohen, and P. Wright. 1989. *Providing Supportive Services to the Frail Elderly in Federally Assisted Housing,* Report 89–2. Washington, D.C.: The Urban Institute Press.

Tuccillo, J. and J. Goodman. 1983. *Housing Finance: A Changing System in the Reagan Era.* Washington, D.C.: The Urban Institute Press.

United Nations. 1982. "Report on the World Health Organizations." Paper presented at the World Assembly on Aging, Vienna, July 26–August 6.

U.S. House Subcommittee on Health and Long-Term Care (1989). *Board and Care Homes in America: A National Tragedy.* Washington, D.C.: U.S. Government Printing Office.

Voeks, S. and P. Drinka. 1990. "Participants' Perception of a Work Therapy Program in a Nursing Home." *Activities, Adaptations and Aging* 14(3):27 - 34.

Weal, F. and F. Weal. 1988. *Housing for the Elderly: Options and Design.* New York: Nichols.

Welch, P., V. Parker, and J. Zeisel. 1984. *Independence Through Interdependence.* Boston: Department of Elder Affairs, Commonwealth of Massachusetts.

Wilner, M. 1988. "Refining the Assisted Living Model to Include Persons with Limited Incomes and Smaller Resident Populations." Portland, Oreg.: Milestone Management.

Wilson, K. 1990. "Assisted Living: The Merger of Housing and Long Term Services." *Long Term Care Advances* (Duke University Center for the Study of Aging and Human Development) 1(4).

Wilson, K. B. 1992. "Management Philosophy: A Critical Element in Implemented Assisted Living." In *Supportive Housing OPTIONS* 1 (1): 11–12. Los Angeles: National Eldercare Institute on Housing and Supportive Services.

Wolfe, D. 1990. *Serving the Ageless Market: Strategies for Selling to the Fifty-plus Market.* New York: McGraw-Hill.

Zeisel, J., G. Epp, and S. Demos. 1977. *Low-Rise Housing for Elderly People: Behavioral Criteria for Design,* #HUD- 483. Washington, D.C.: U.S. Government Printing Office, September.

Index

Note: Italicized page references denote illustrations.